THIS BOOK
BELONGS TO THE
COLLECTION OF

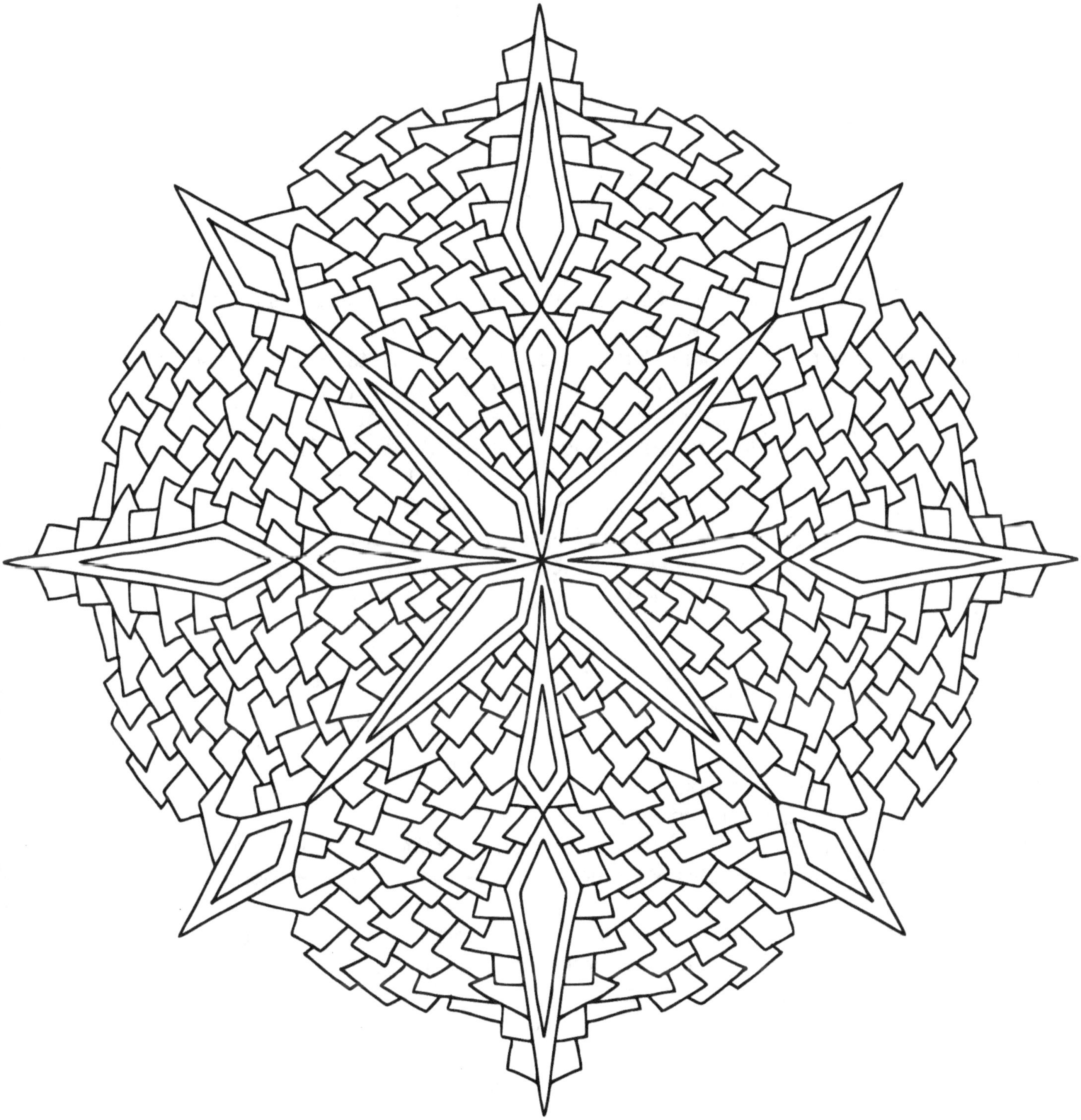

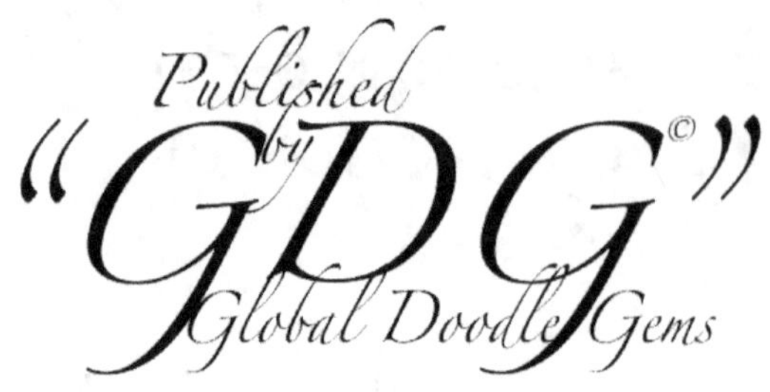

Share your colored versions with us ! We love seeing your results
and hearing from you
we are social !

The Official FB book page, stay on top of what we have in the works !
www.facebook.com/AMVWART
The Community group, share your colored pages, meet the artists, enjoy exclusive freebies, take
part in community Charity books and so much more......
www.facebook.com/groups/fansandfriendsamvwart
www.facebook.com/groups/ColorAWeirdieADay
Follow us on Twitter.... @GlobalDoodlegem
We are on Instagram too
@globaldoodlegems for instagram
...and if you are not social like that we have a blog
globaldoodlegems.wordpress.com

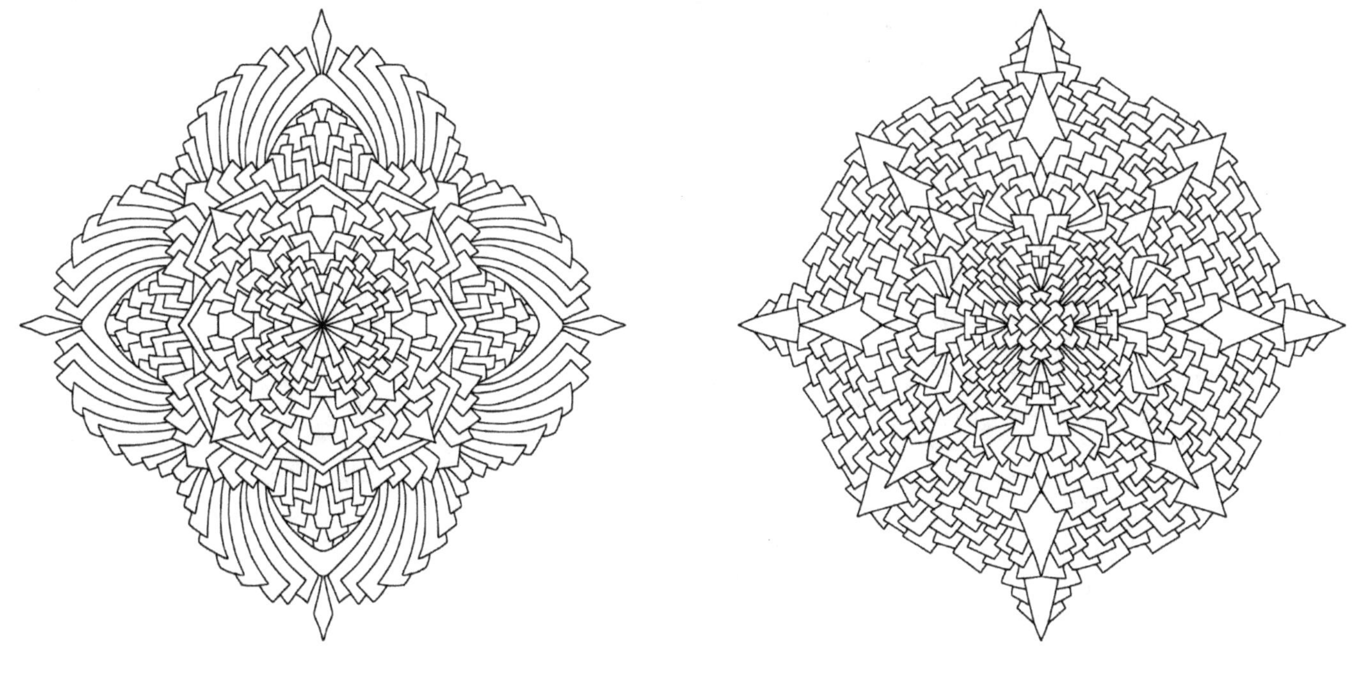

Abstra'Dala's

I hope that you will enjoy this challenging book... it is as easy as you make it or as hard as you set it to be ... only your imaginations set the limits... have fun and enjoy !

"This book is dedicated to the love of my life, my daughter Victoria Panthera. I make these books in hopes that your life as an adult will be everything you want It to be! I love you more than words can say!"

Maria Wedel

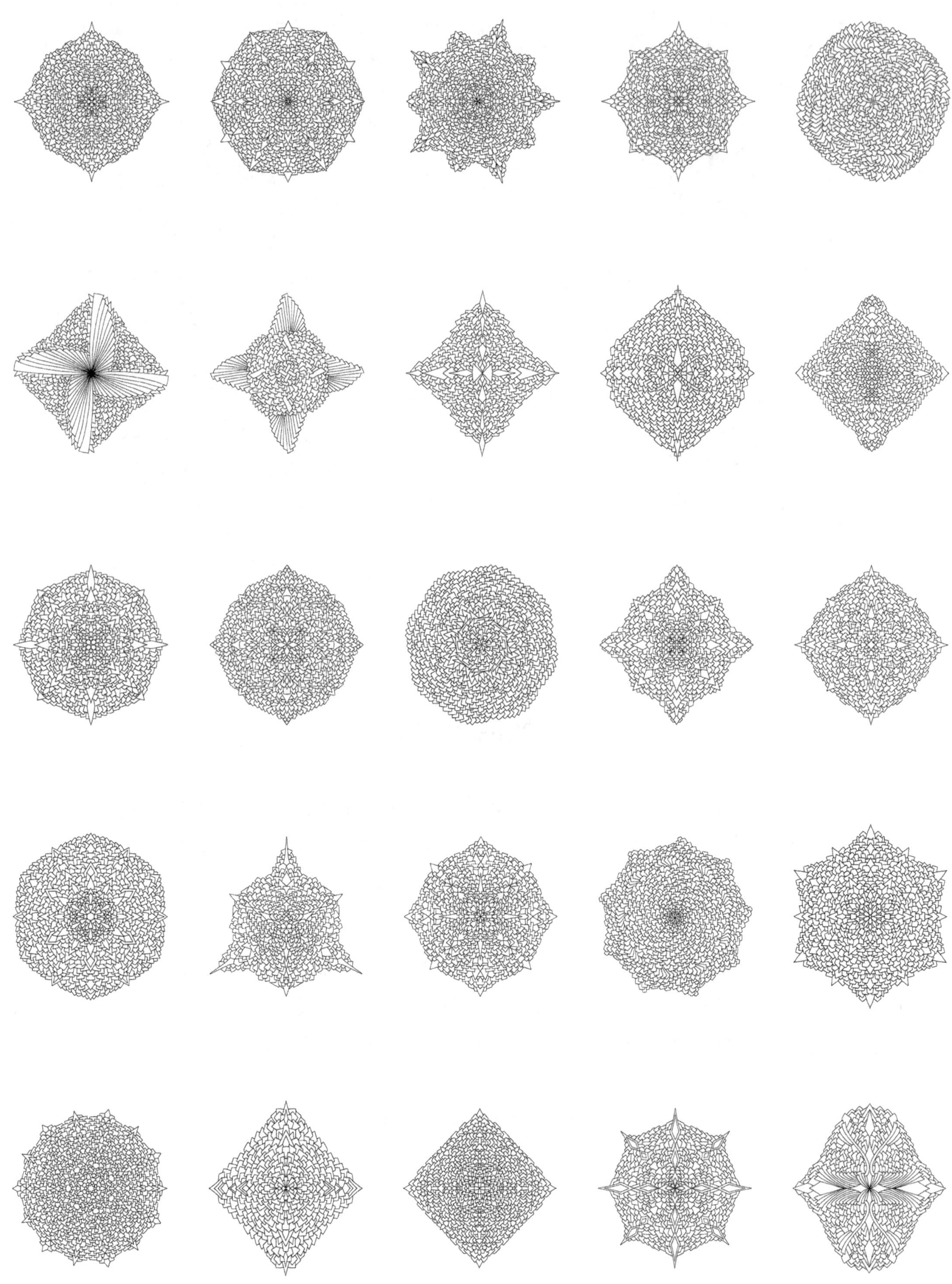

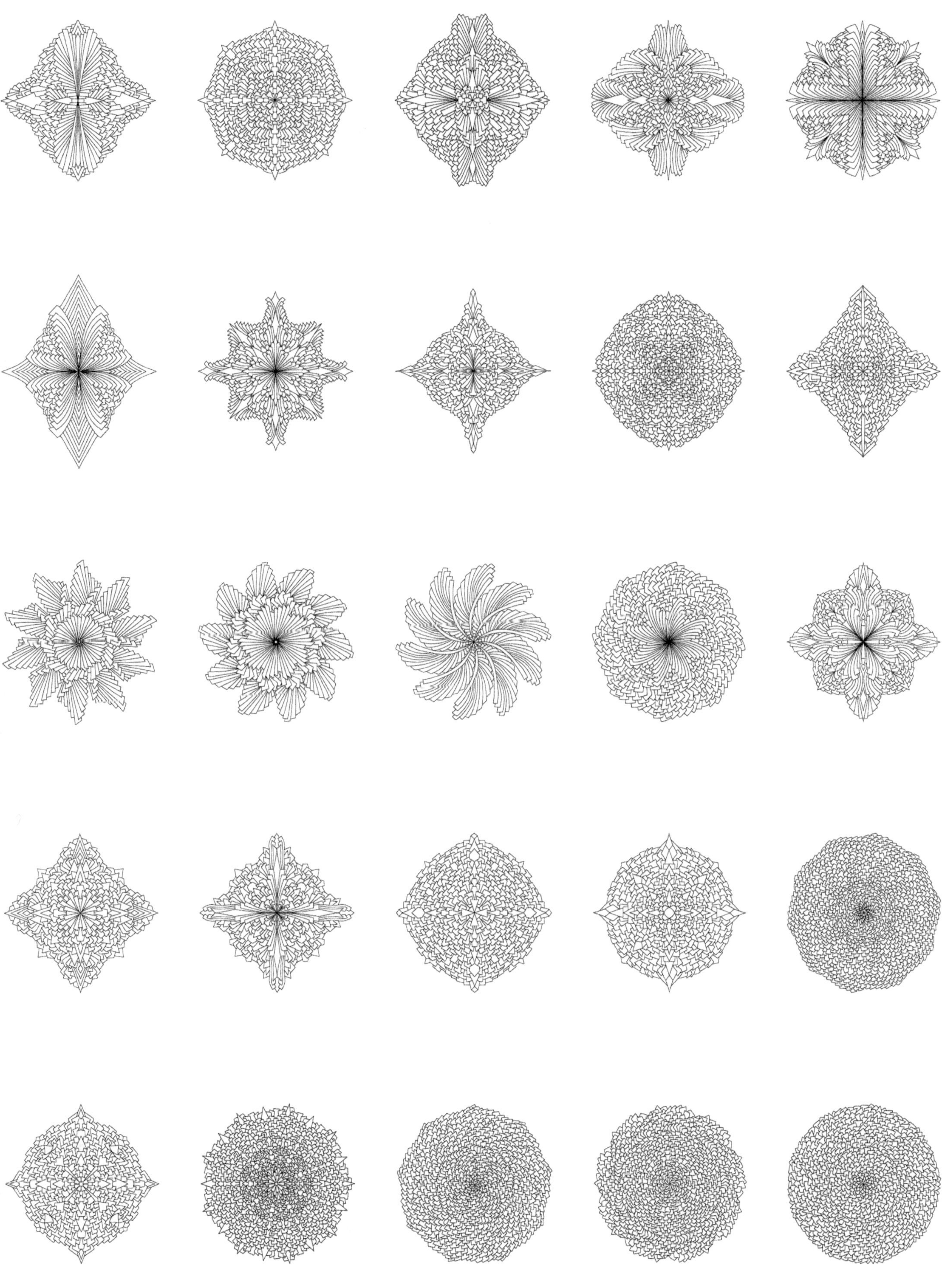

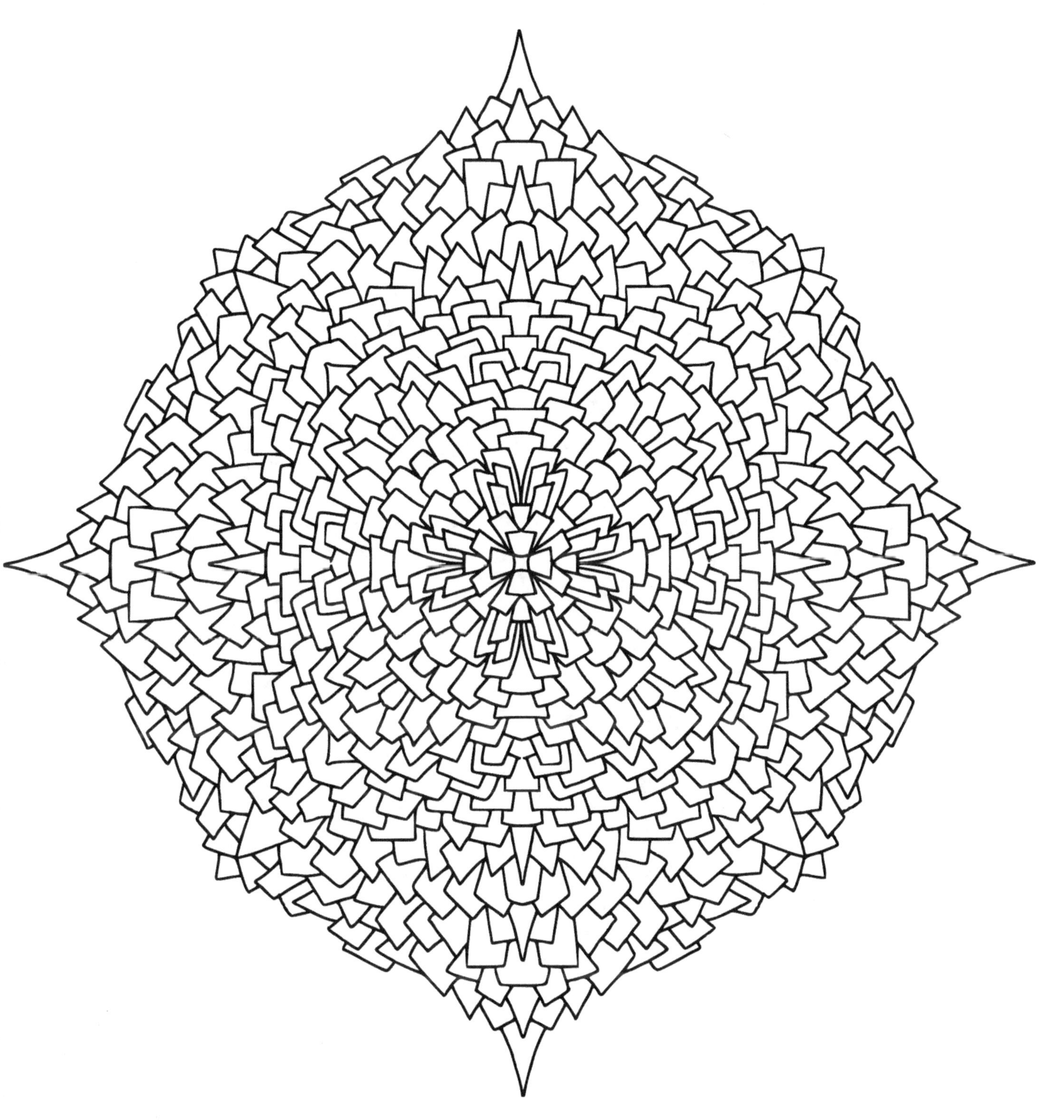

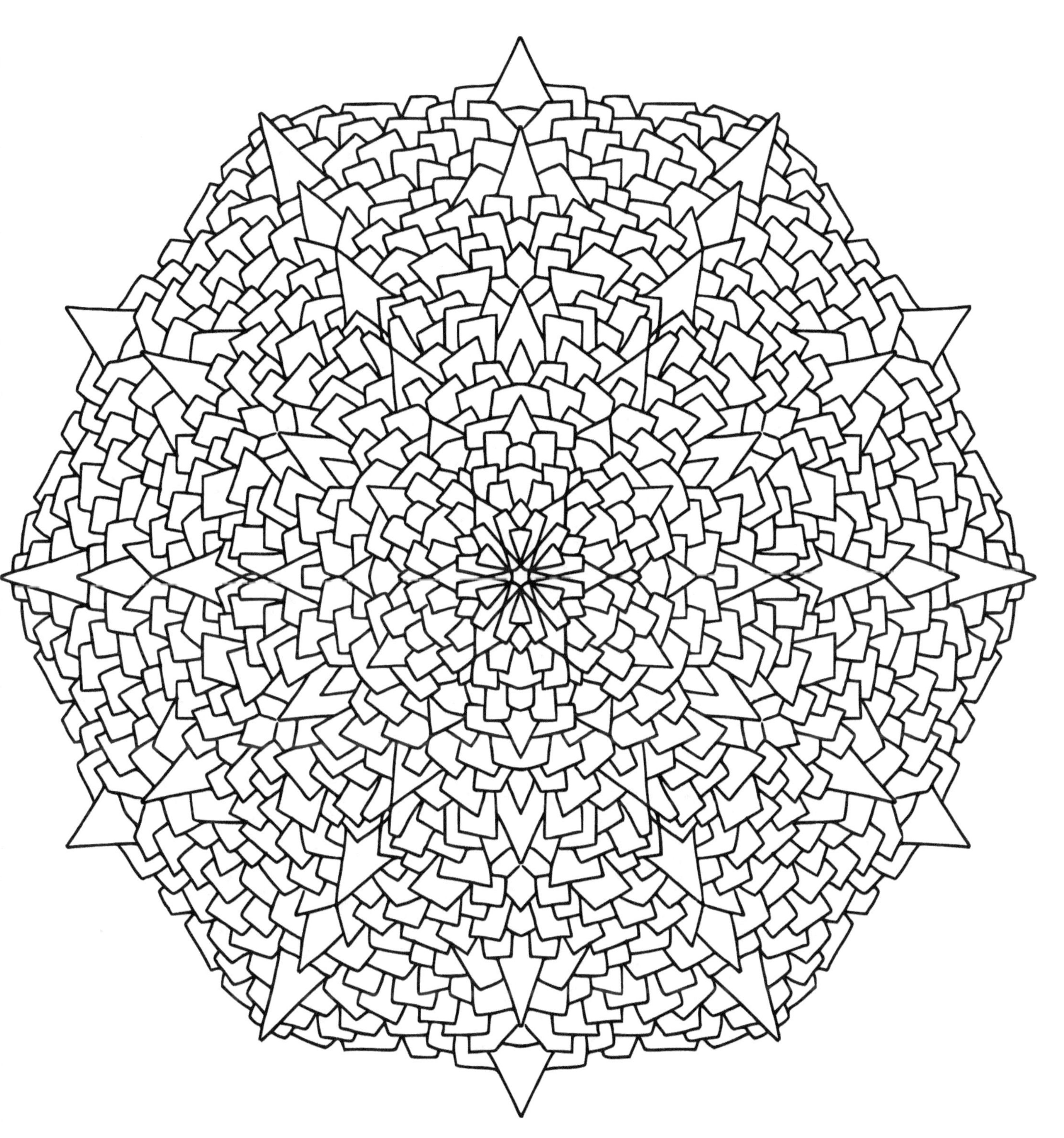

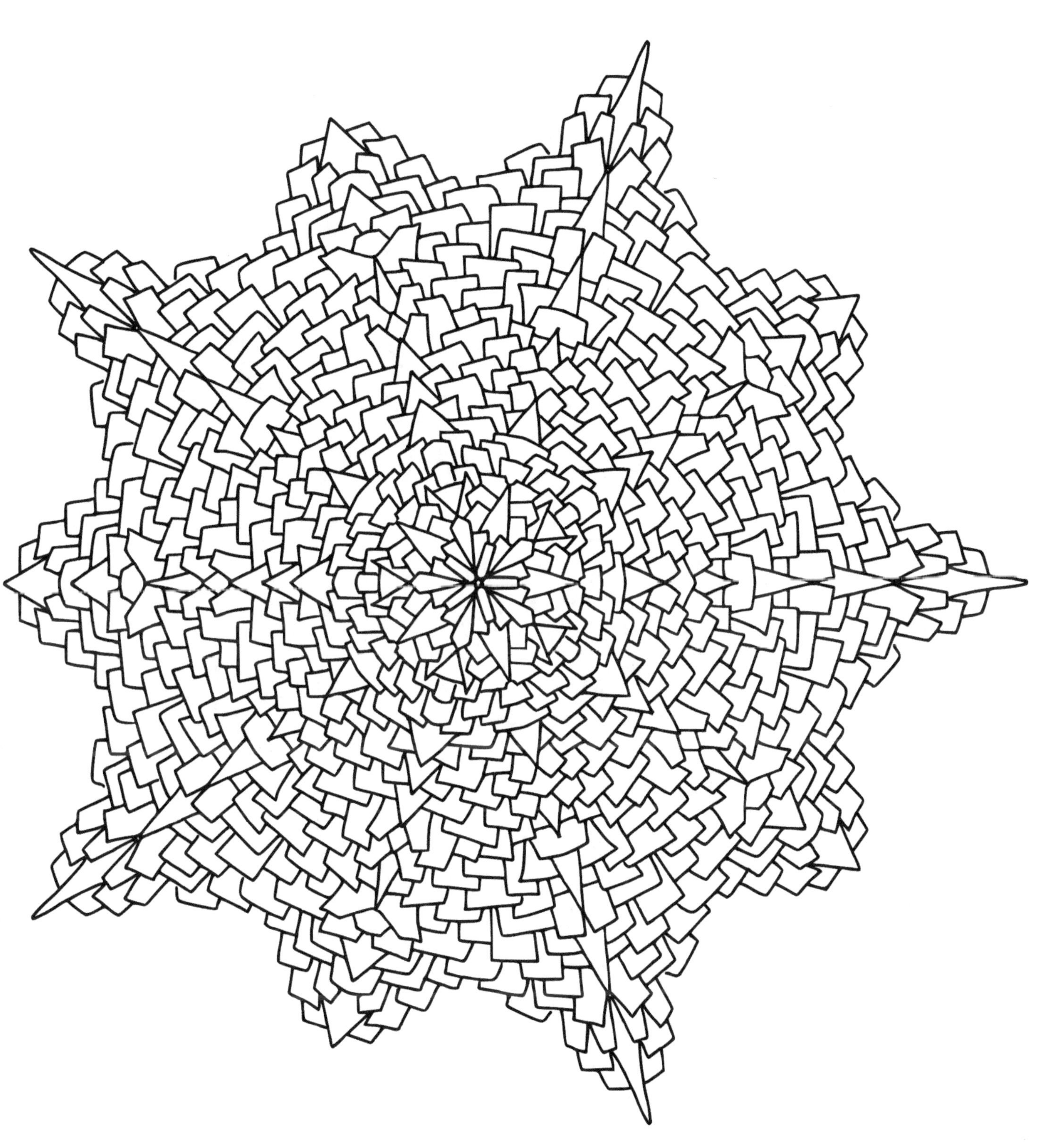

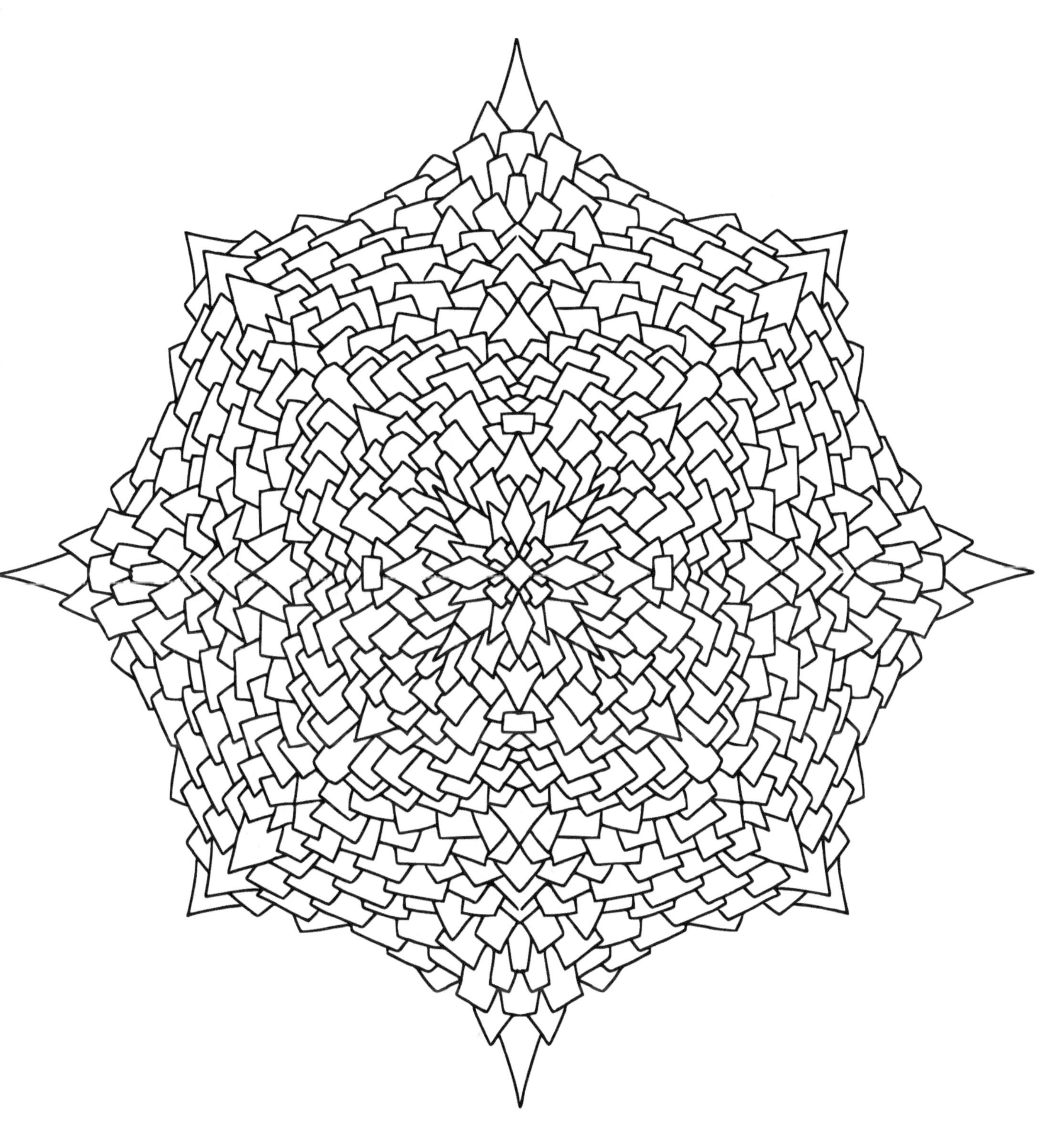

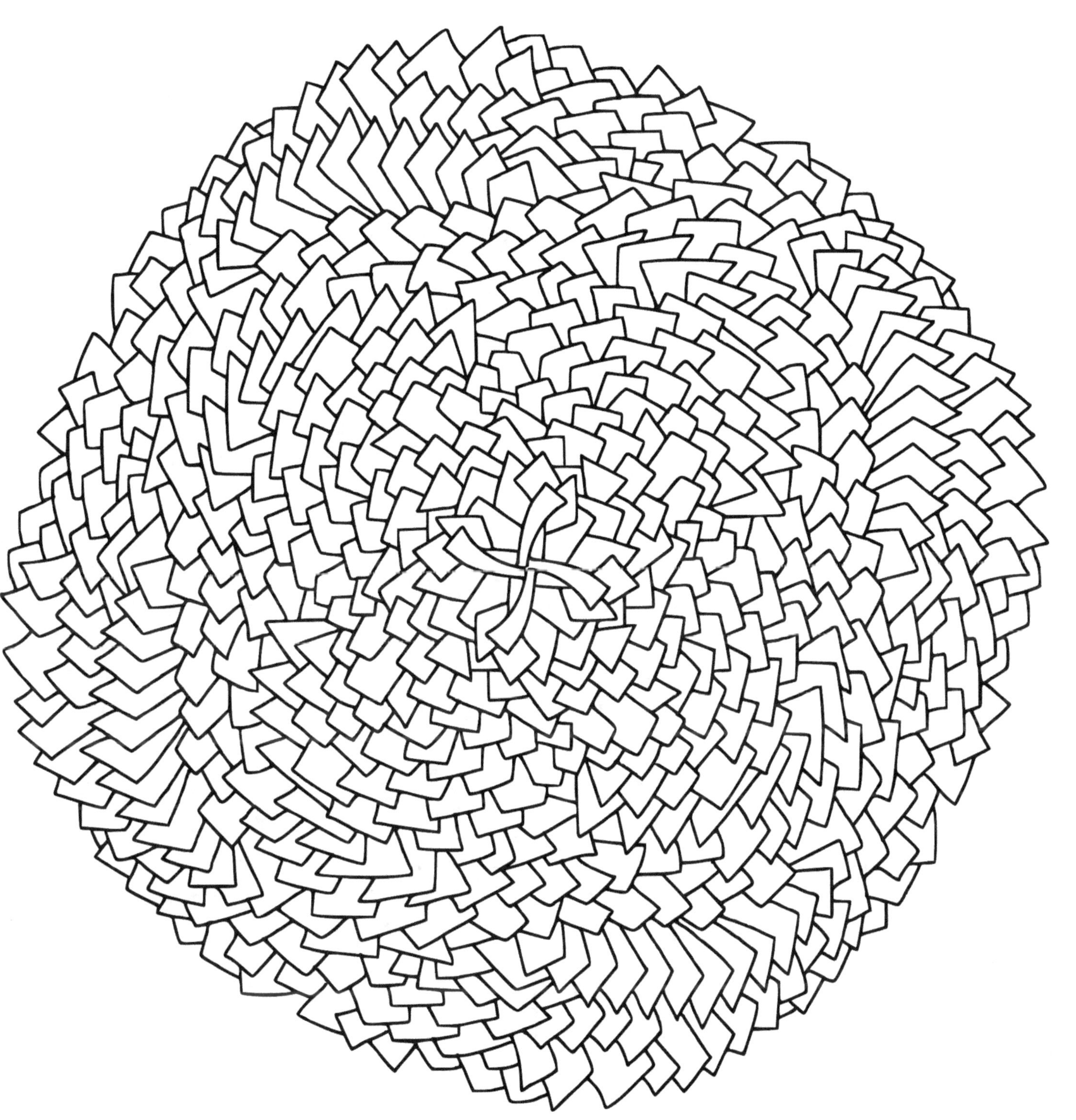

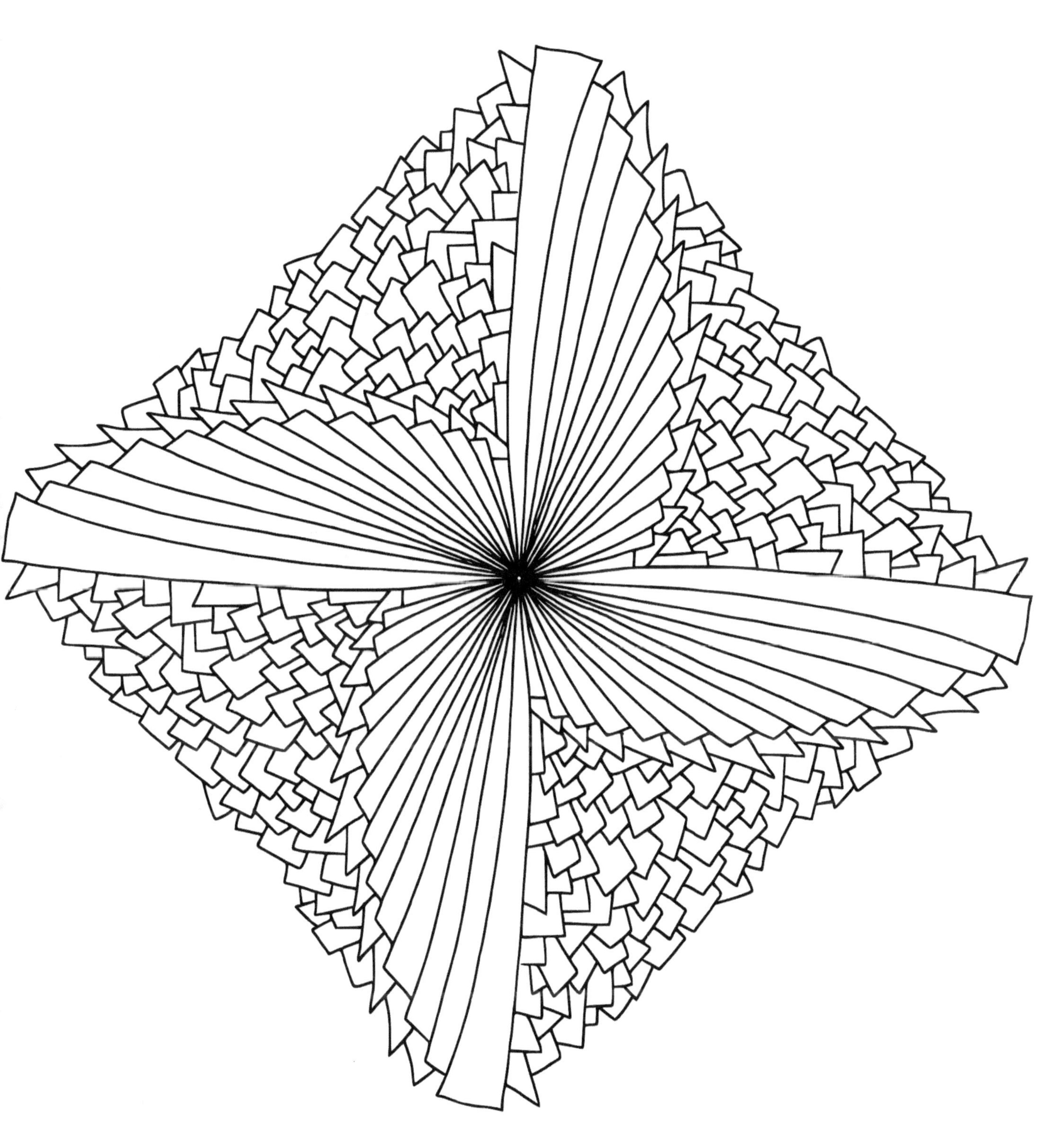

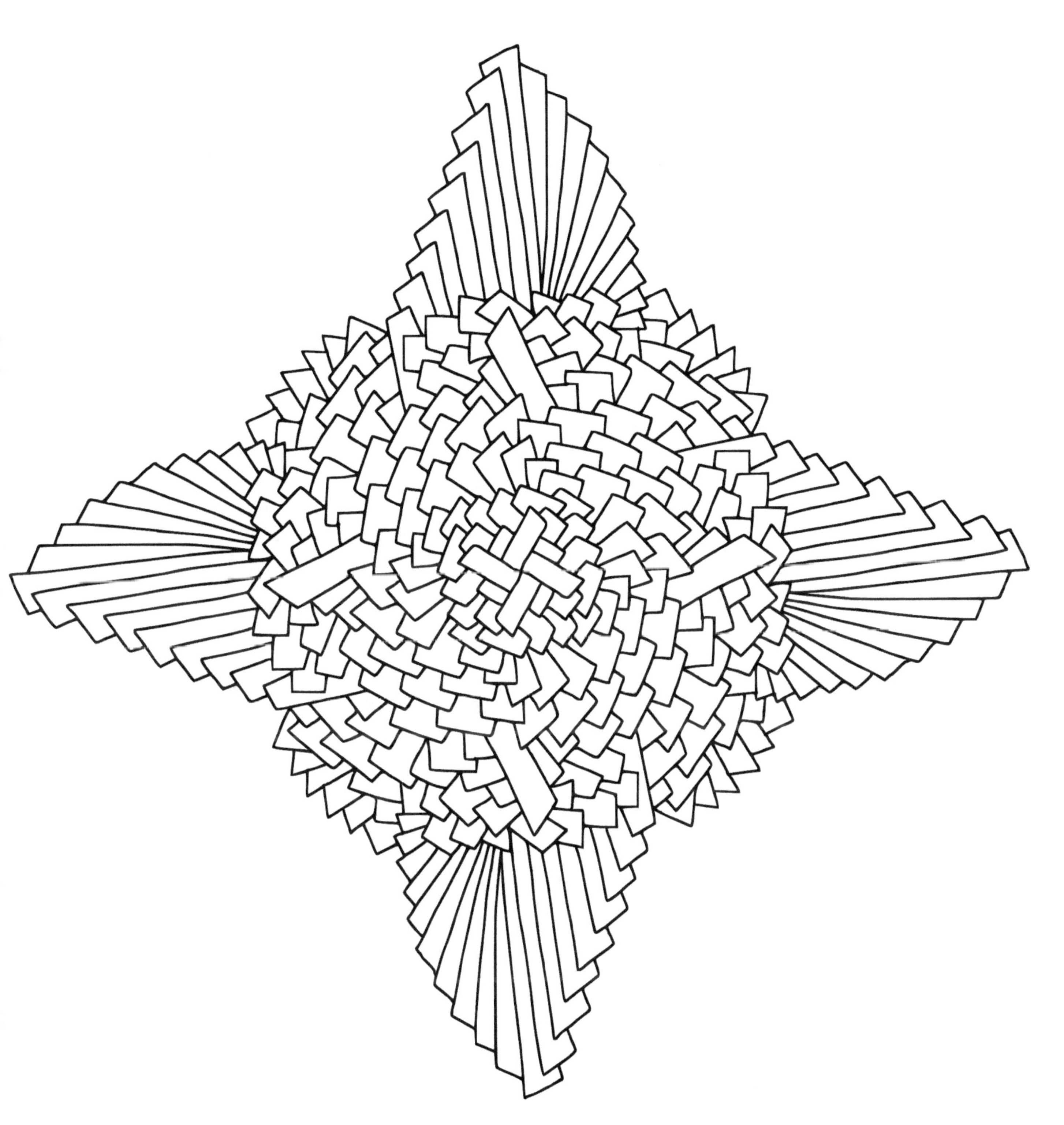

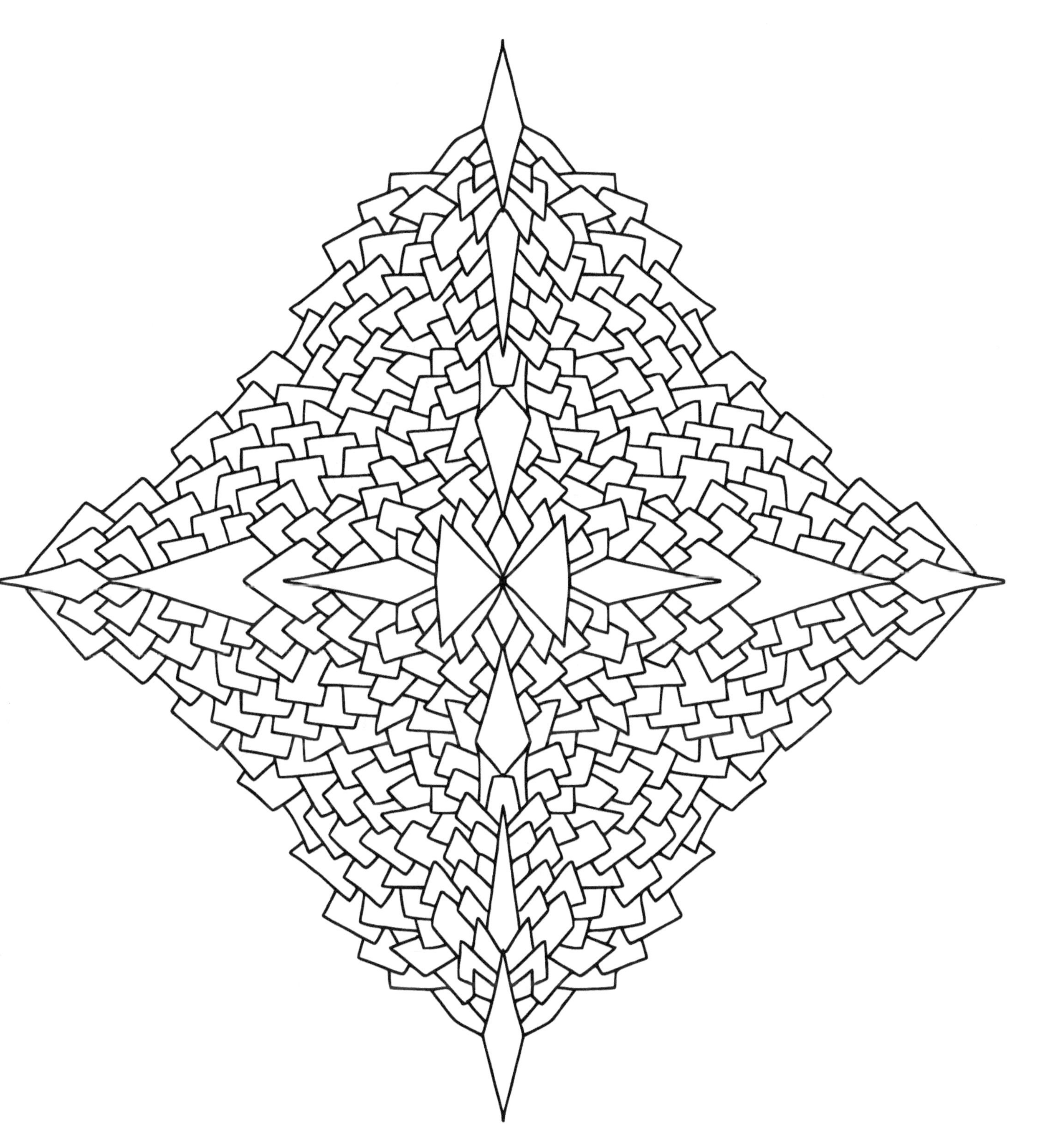

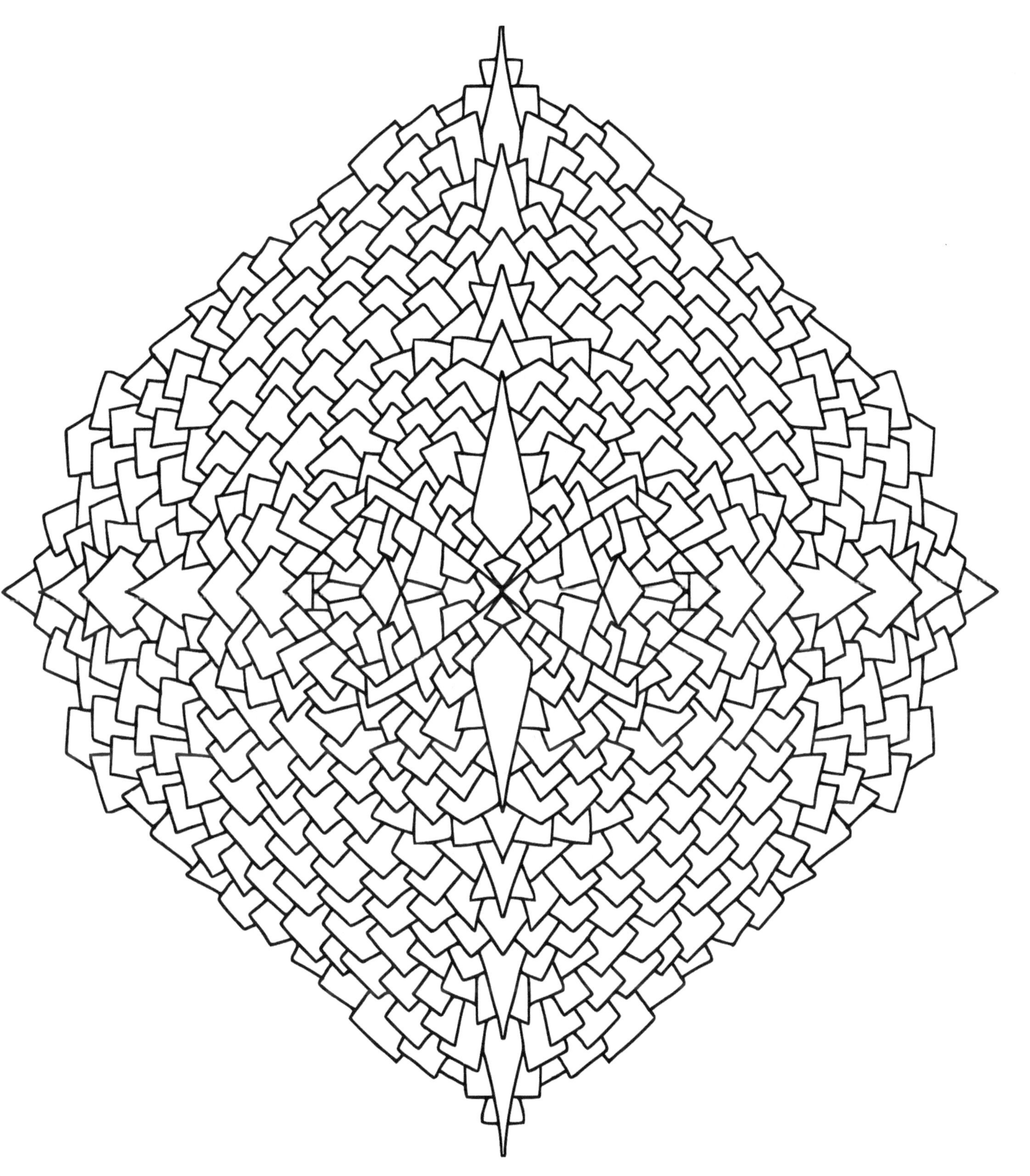

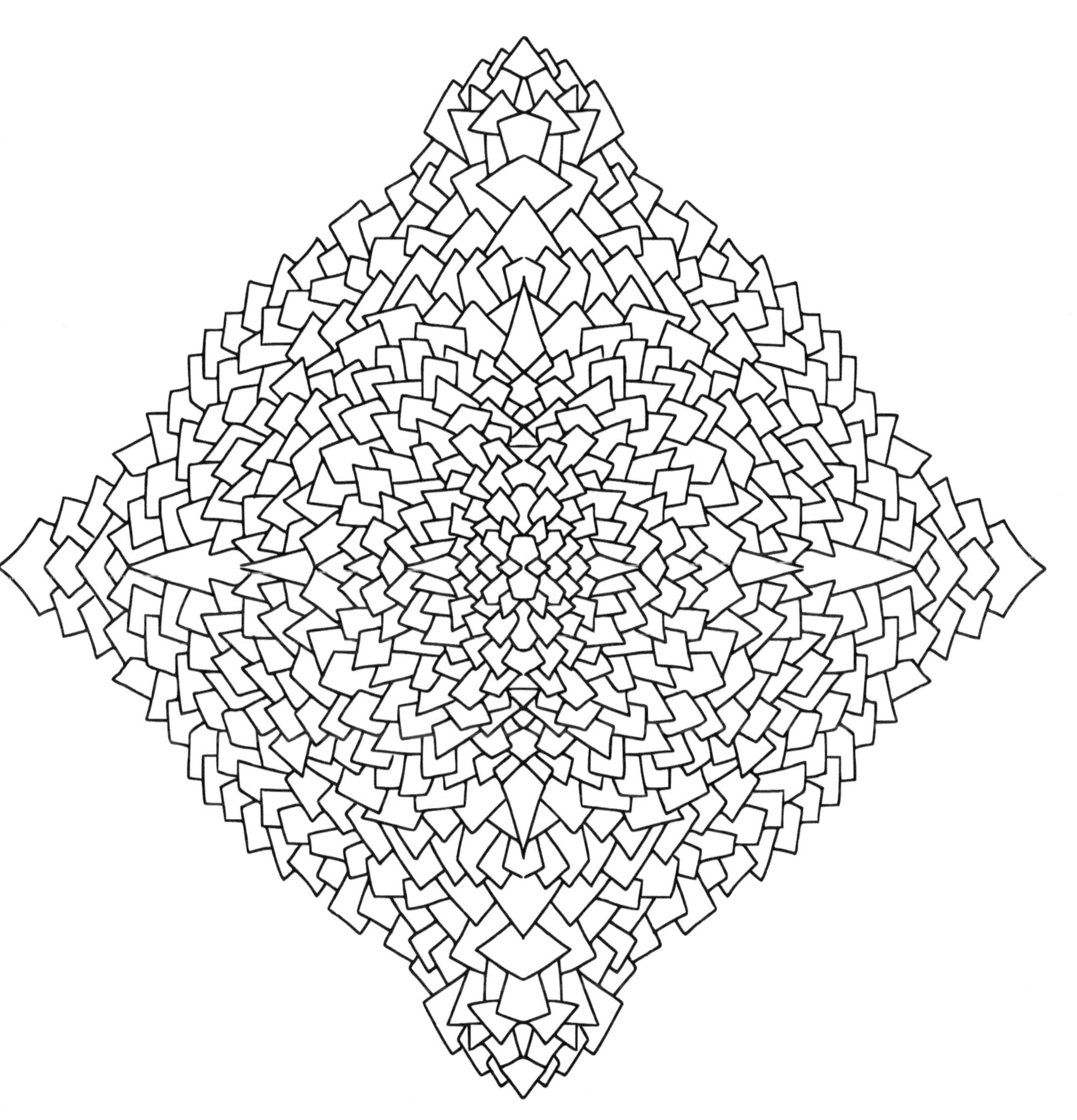

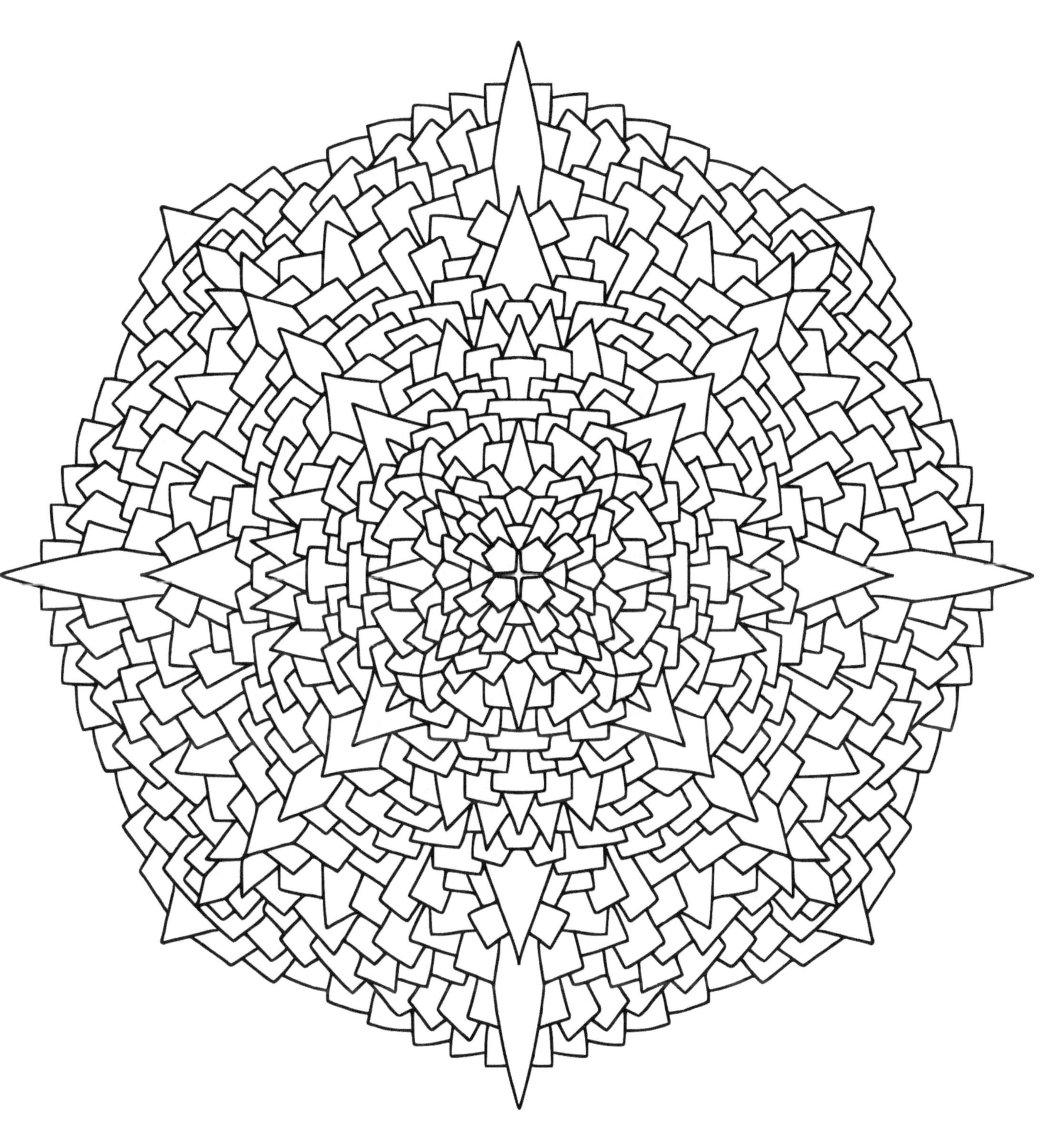

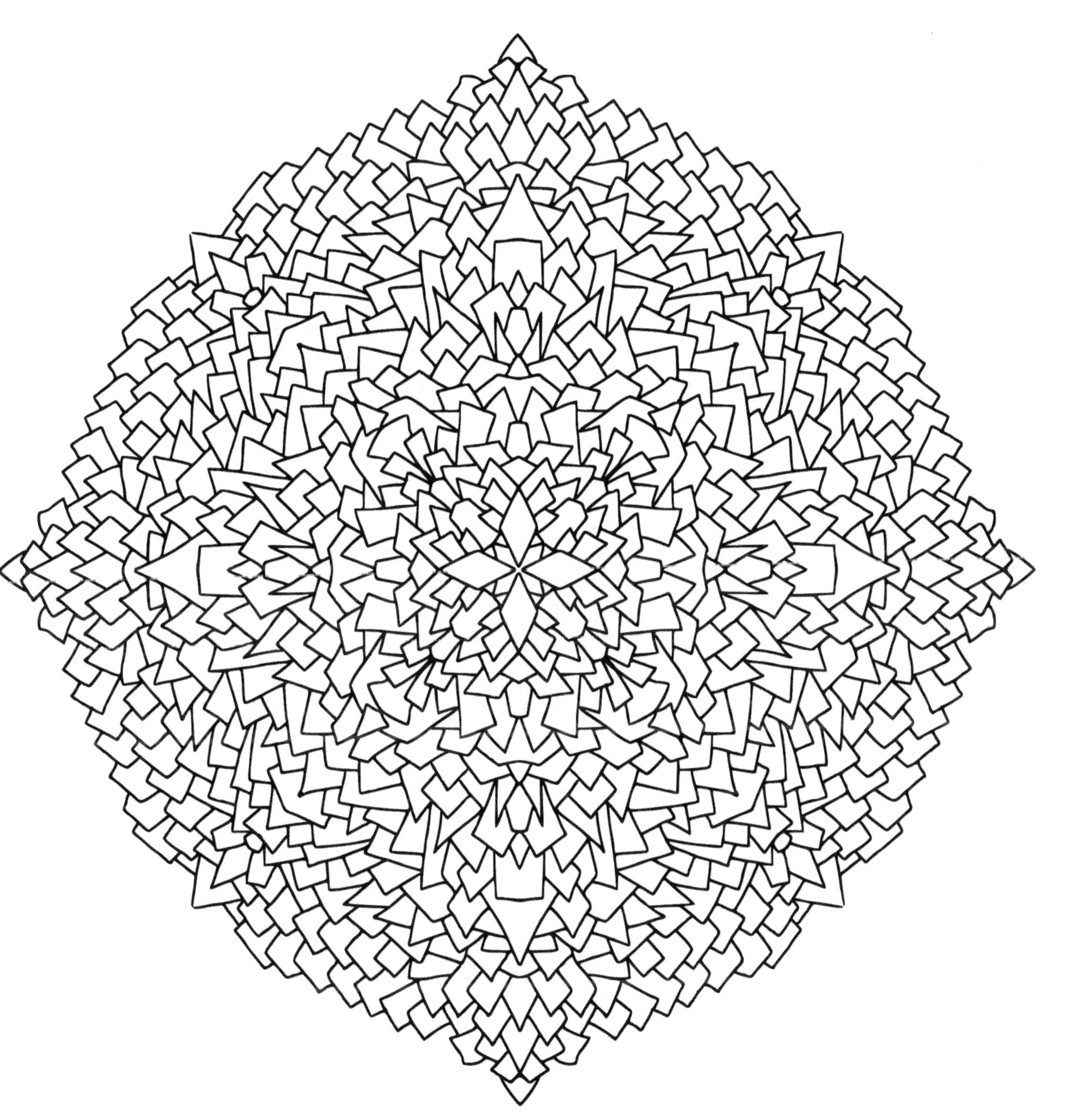

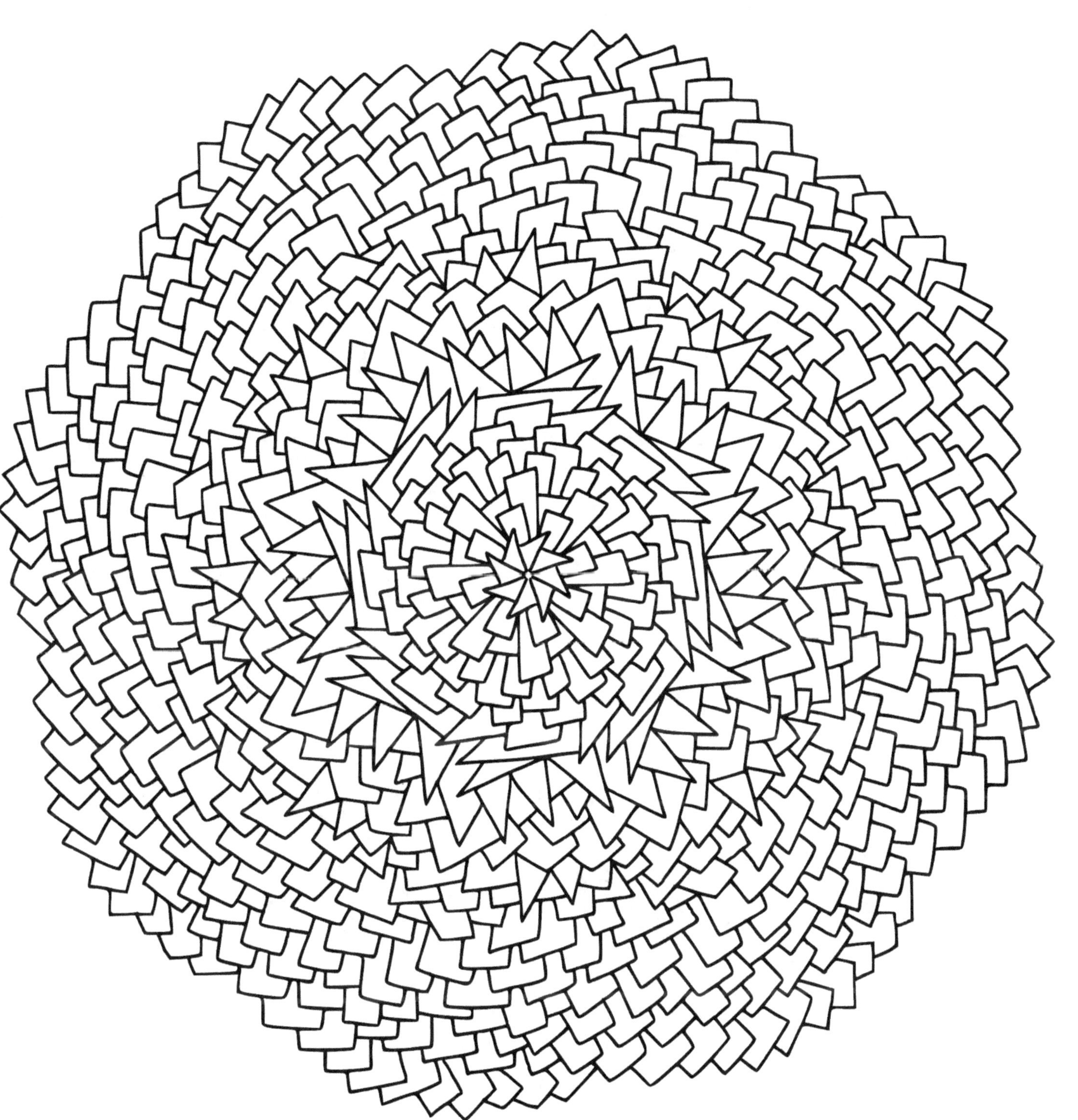

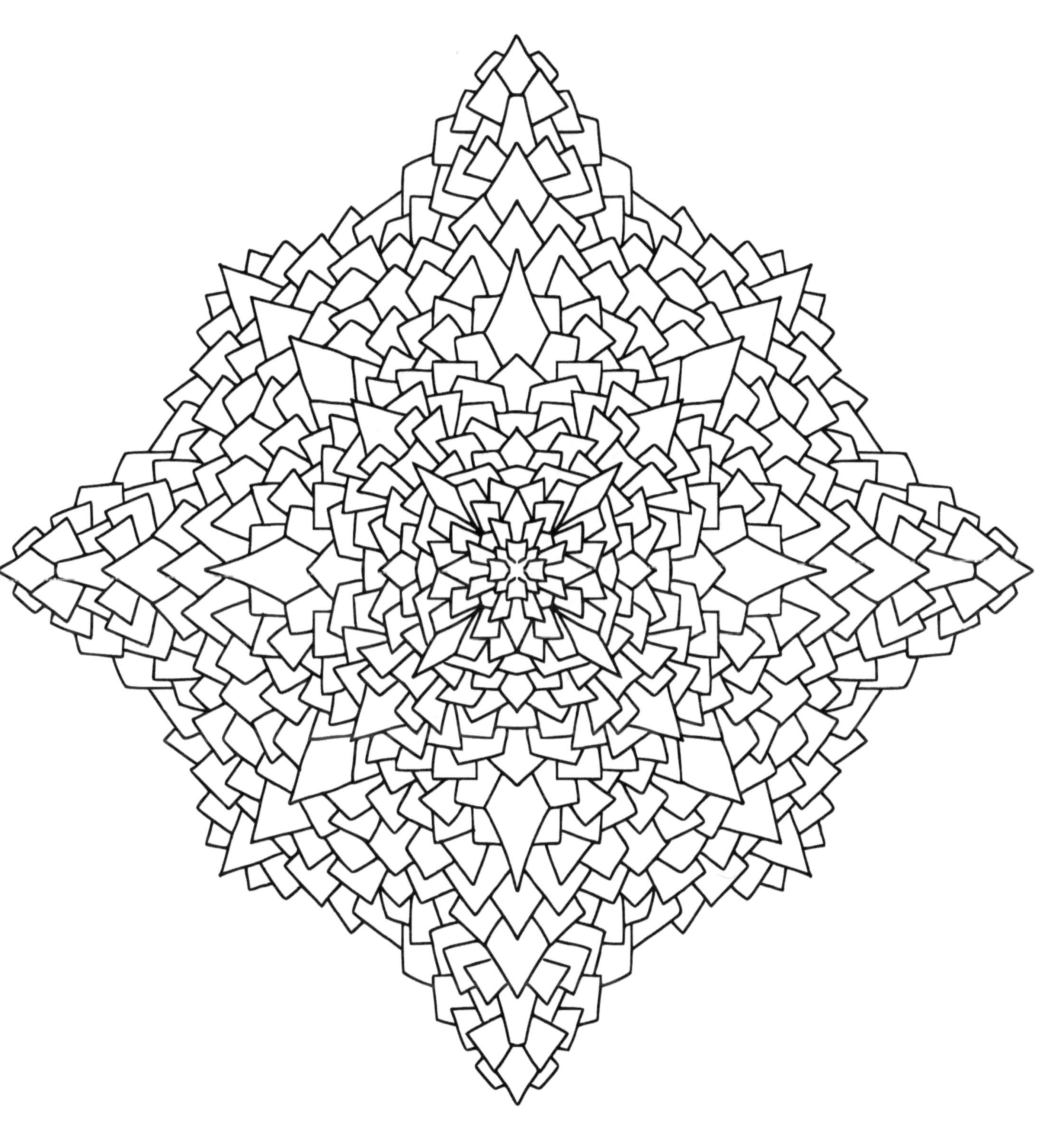

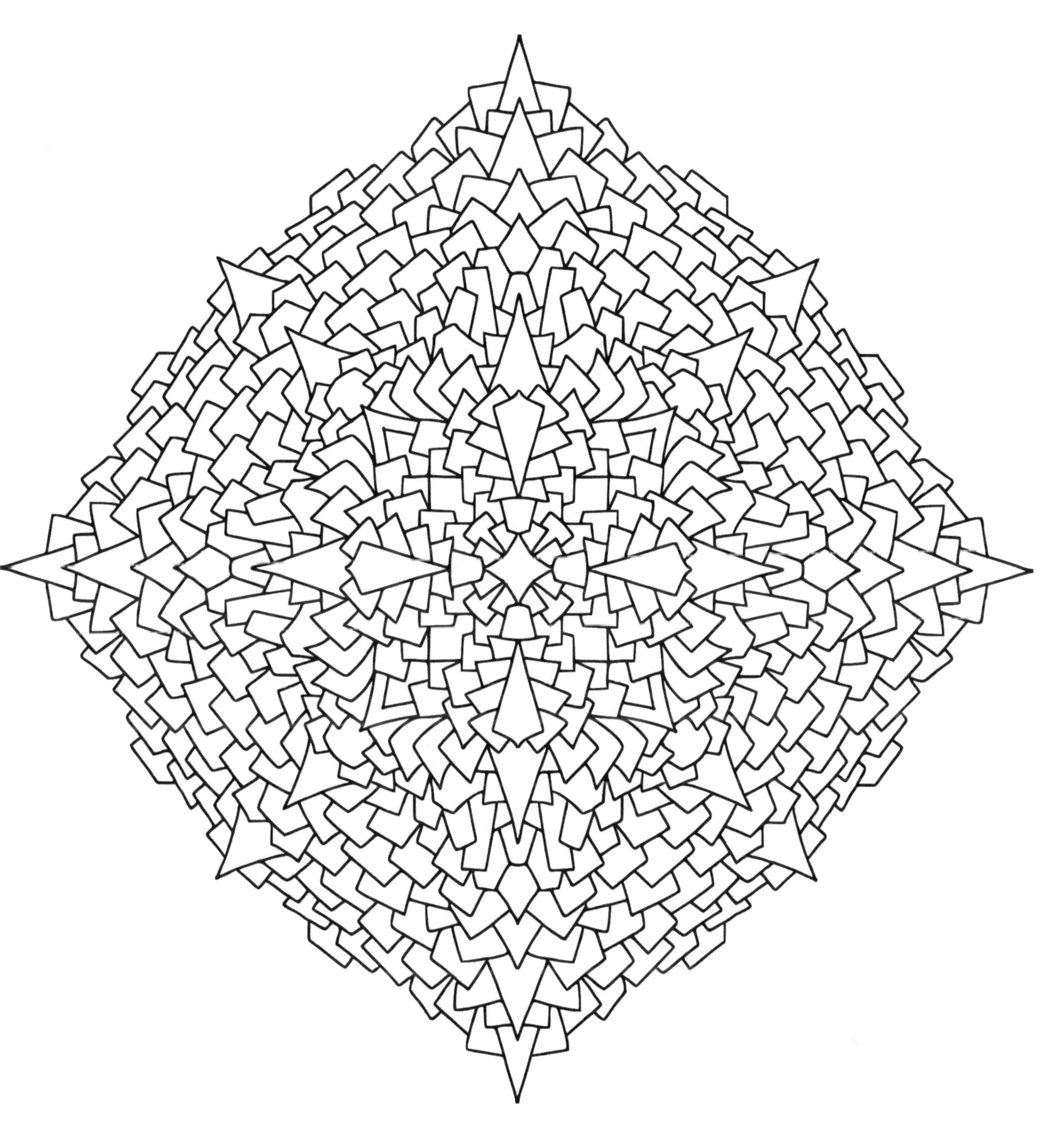

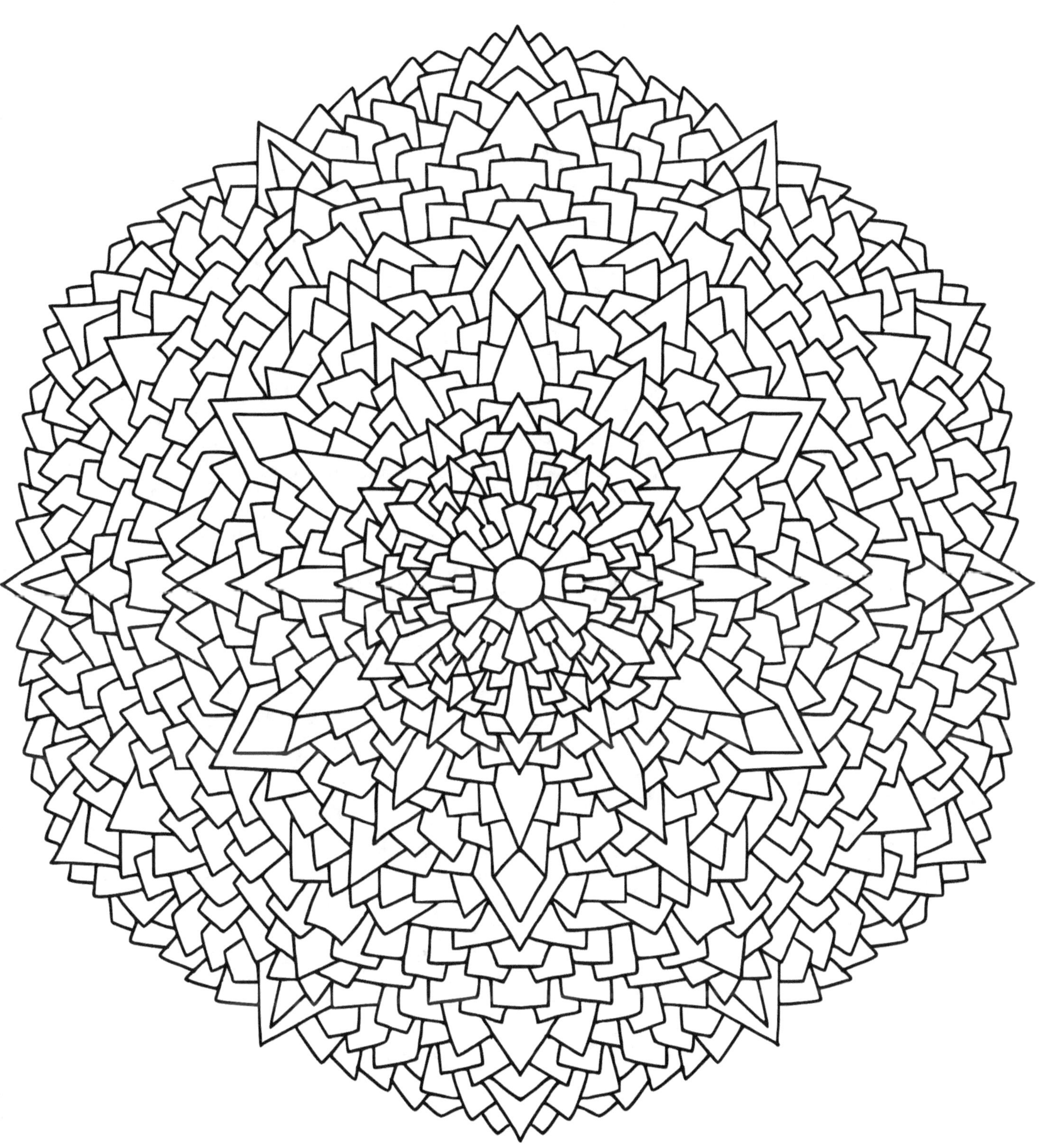

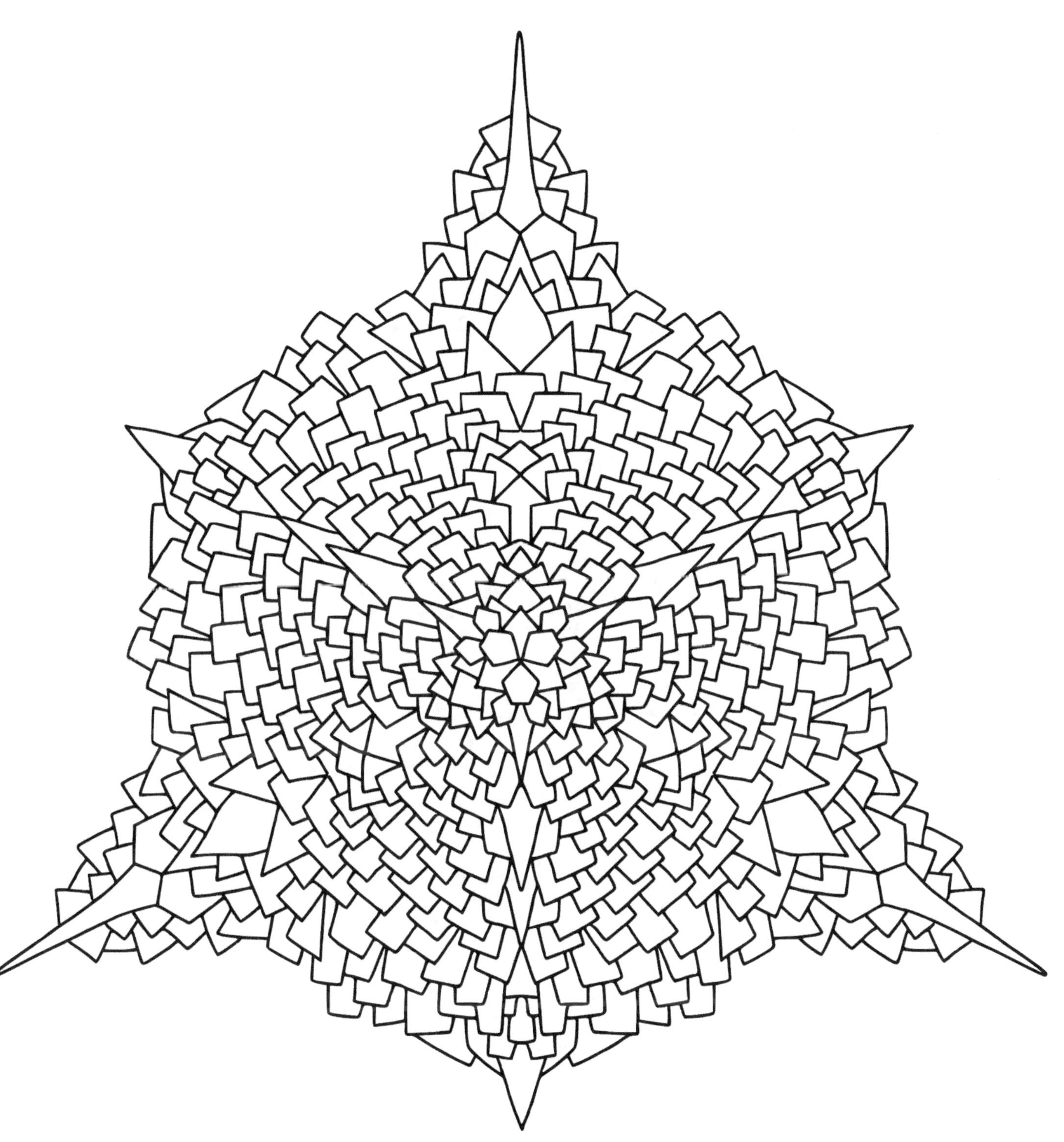

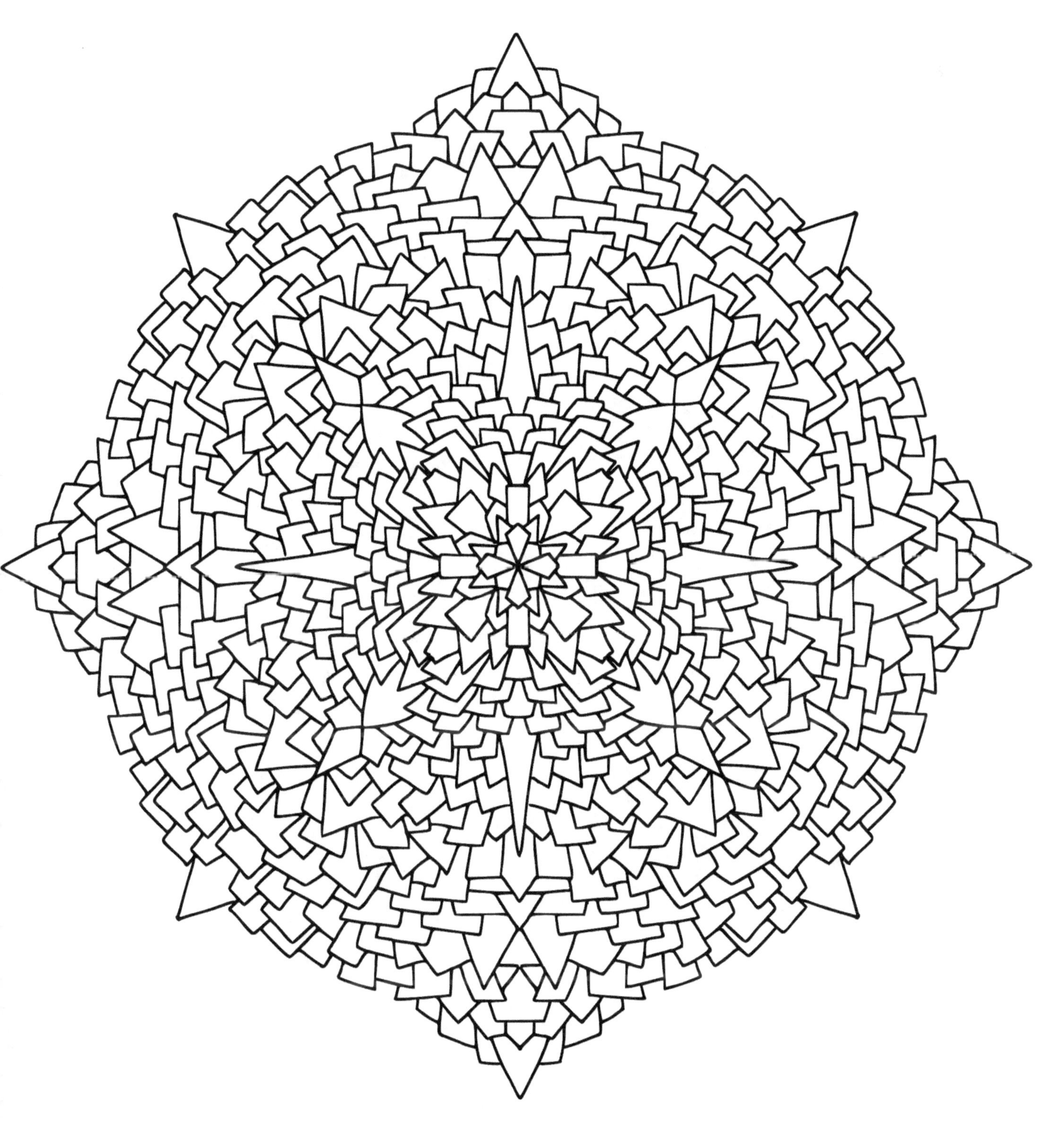

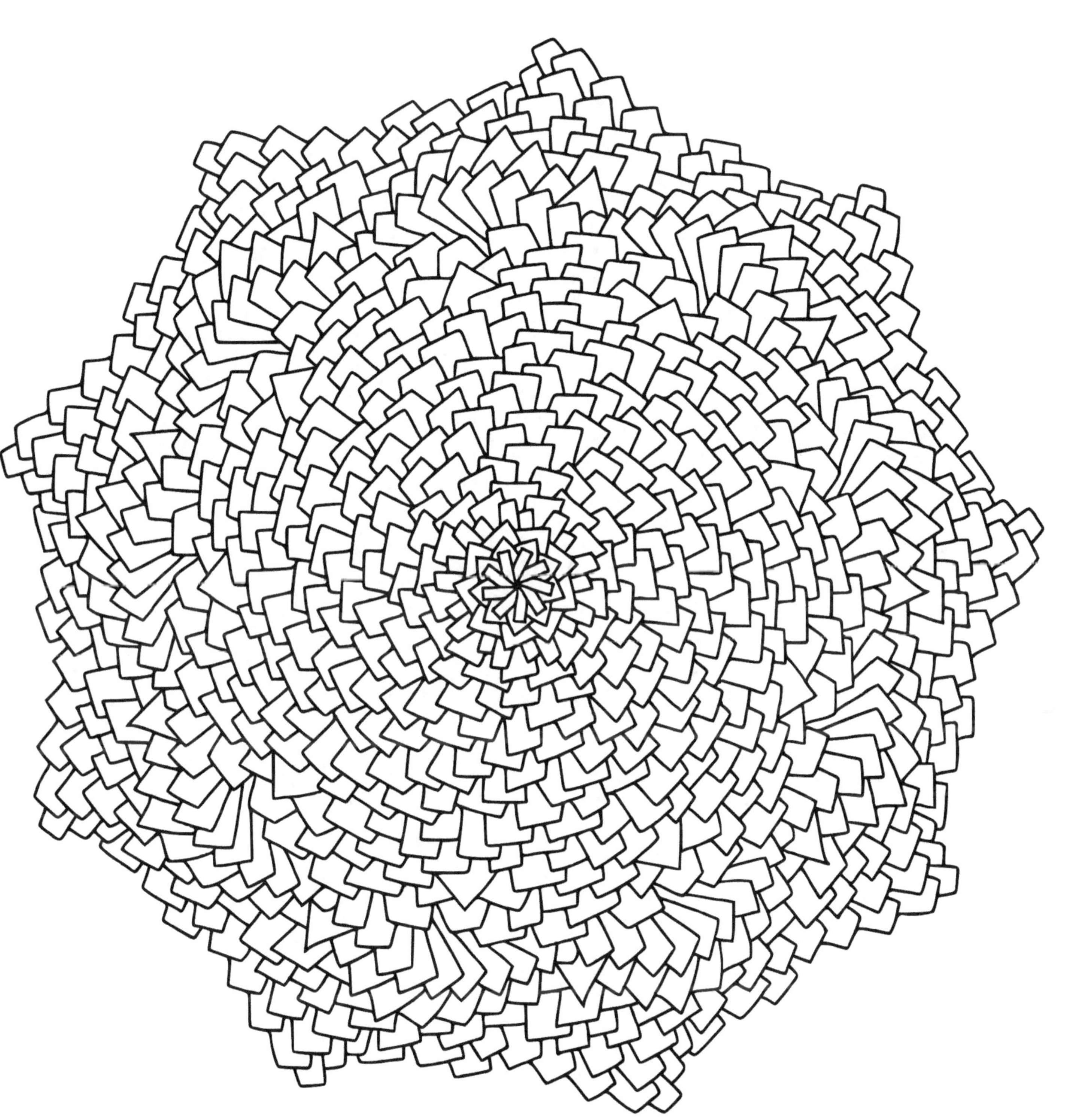

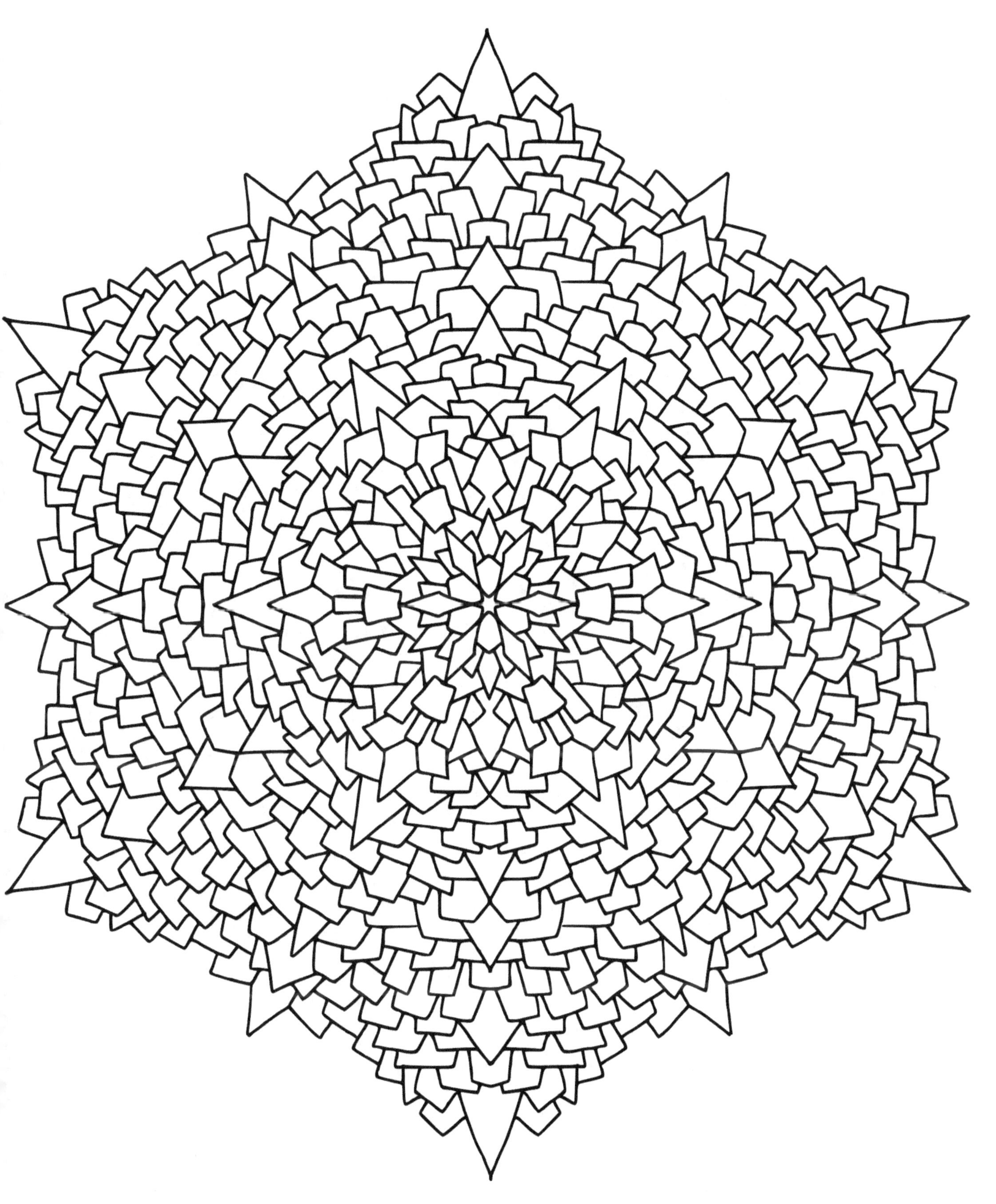

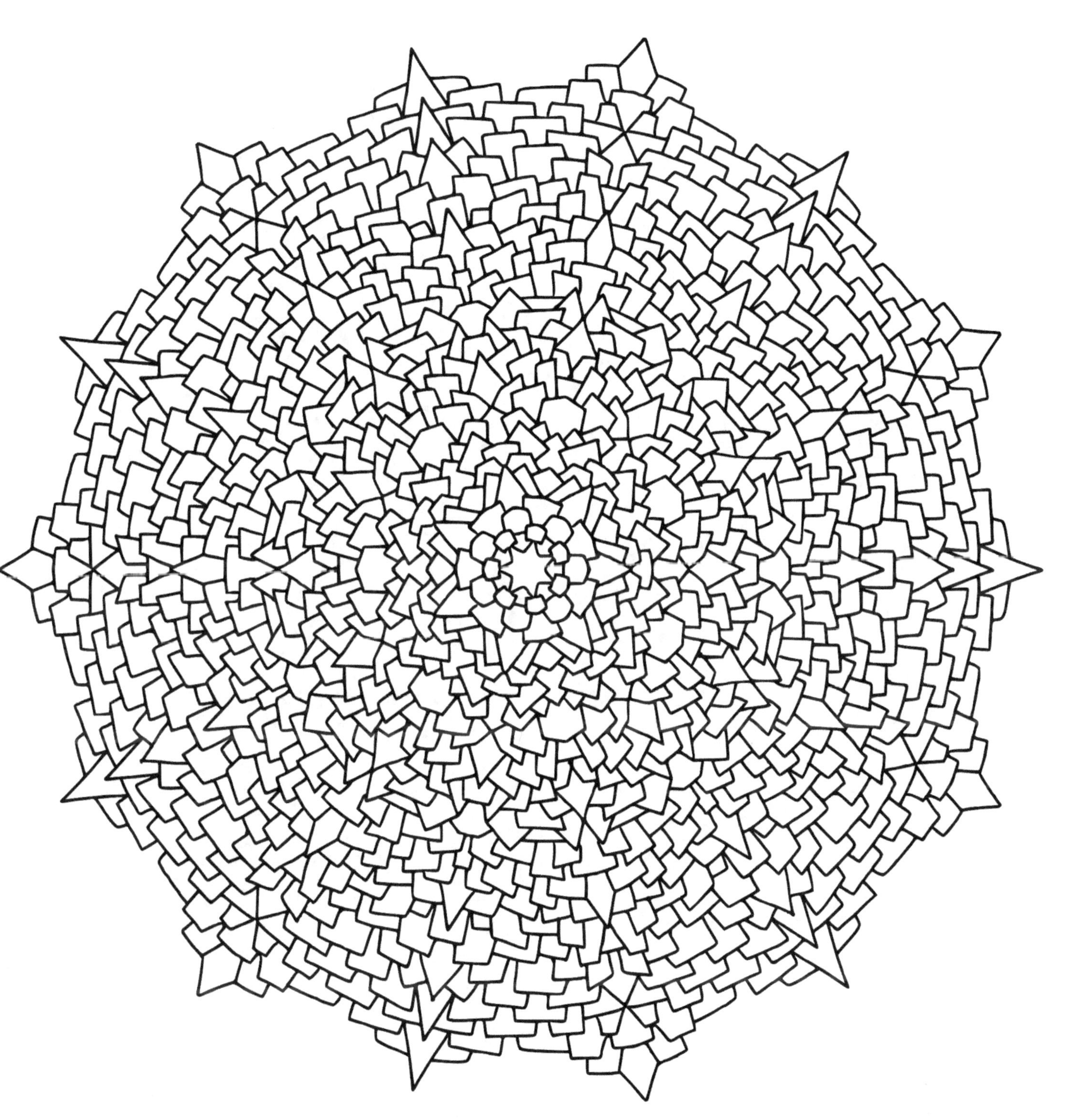

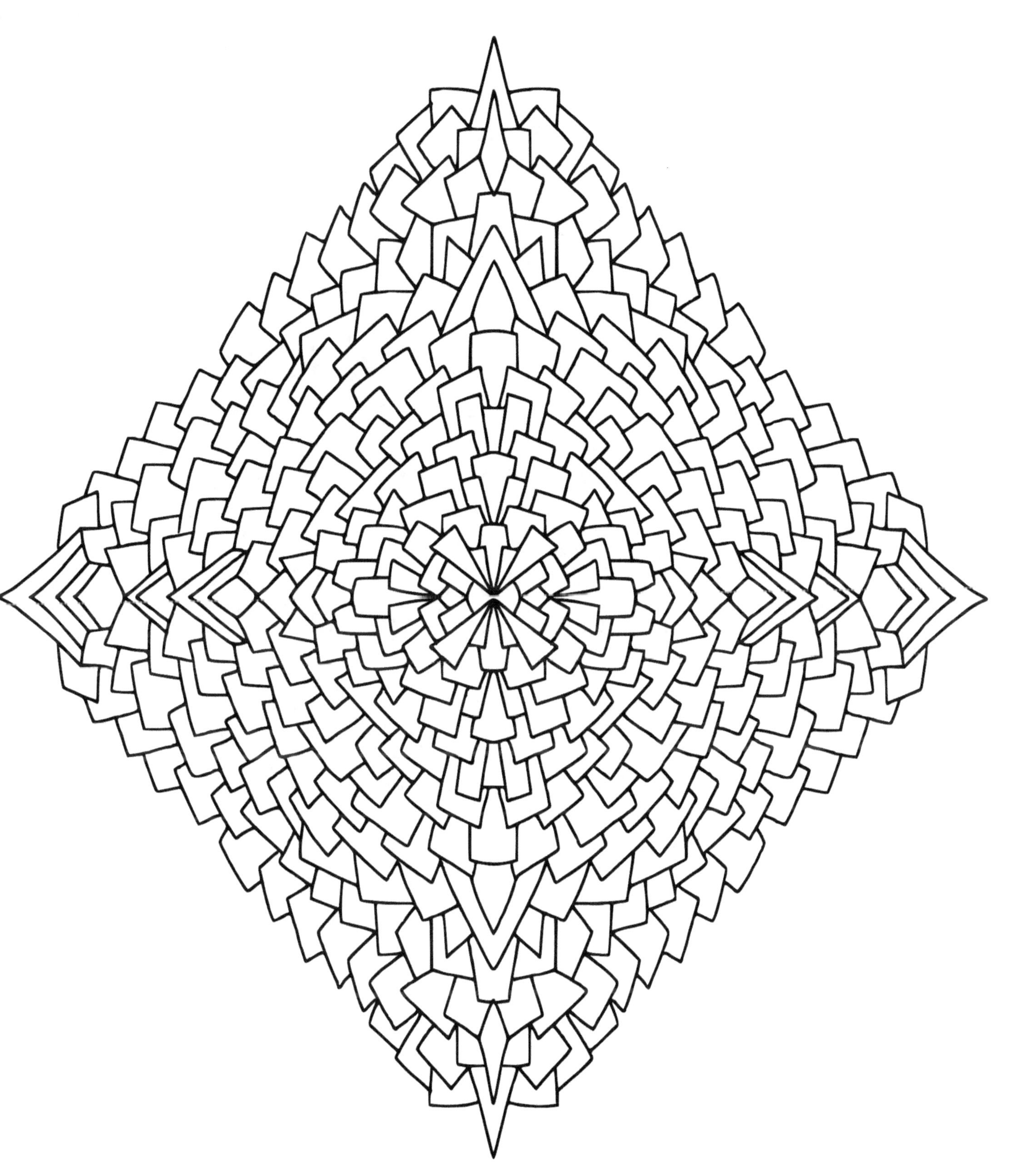

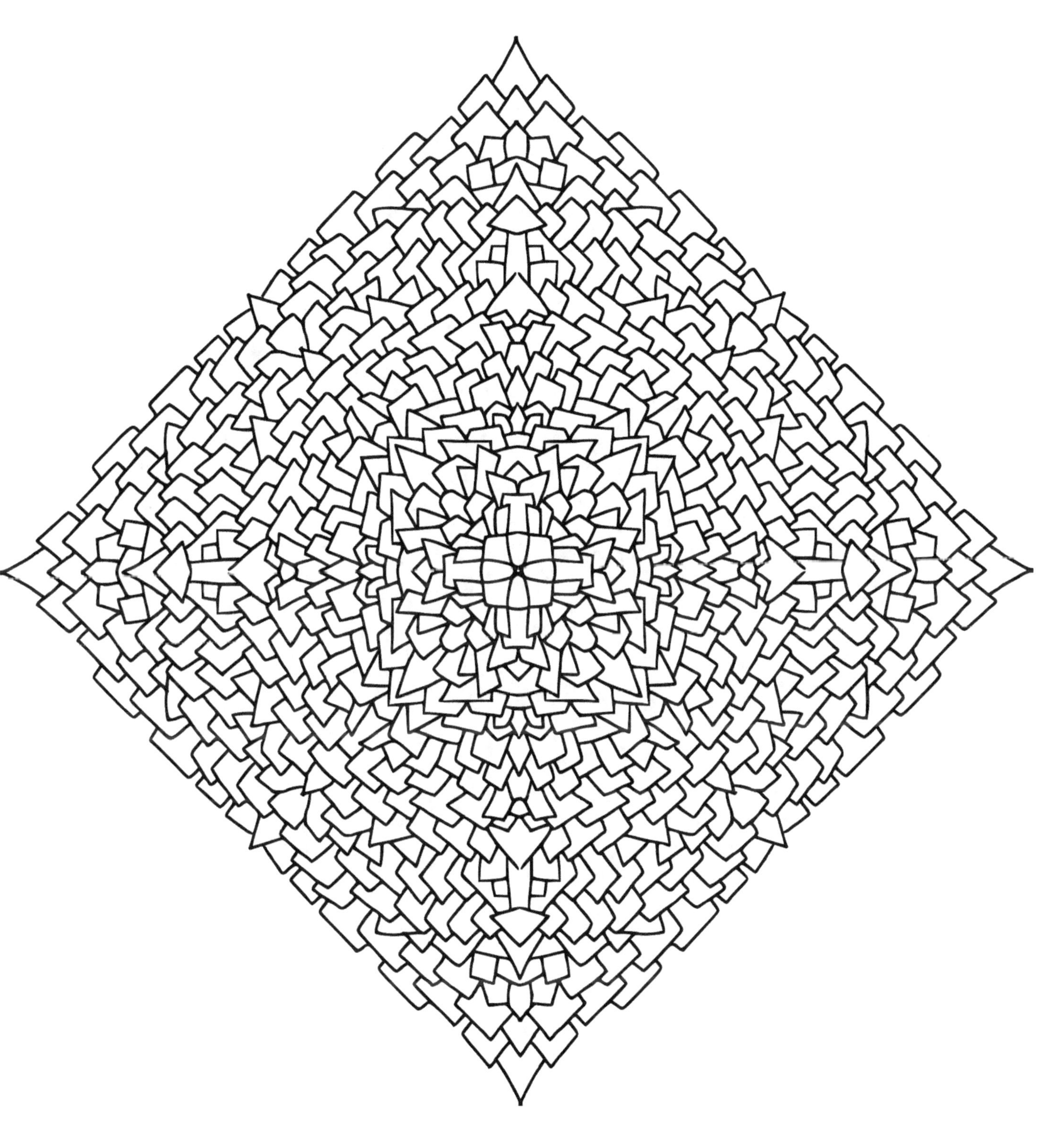

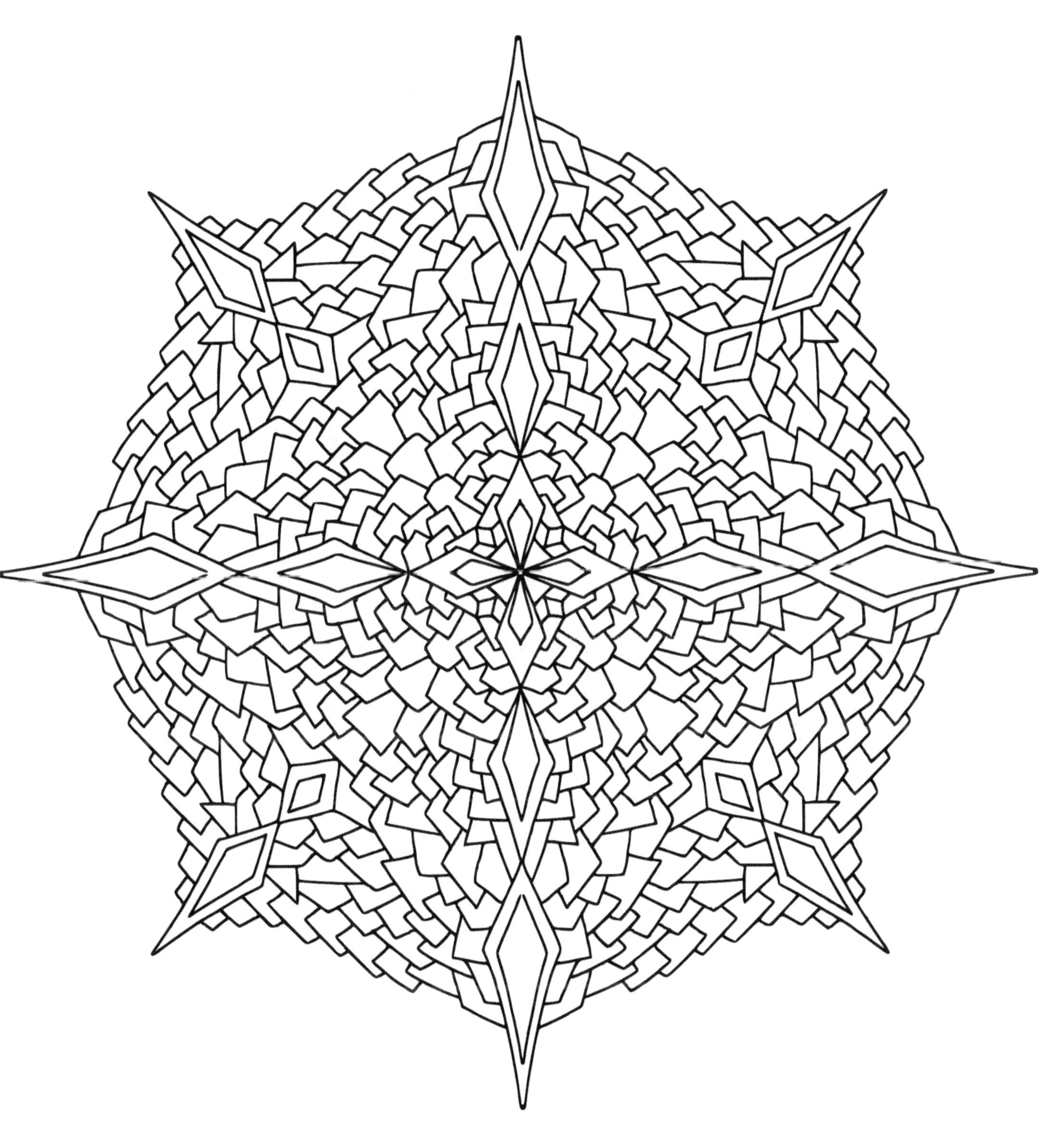

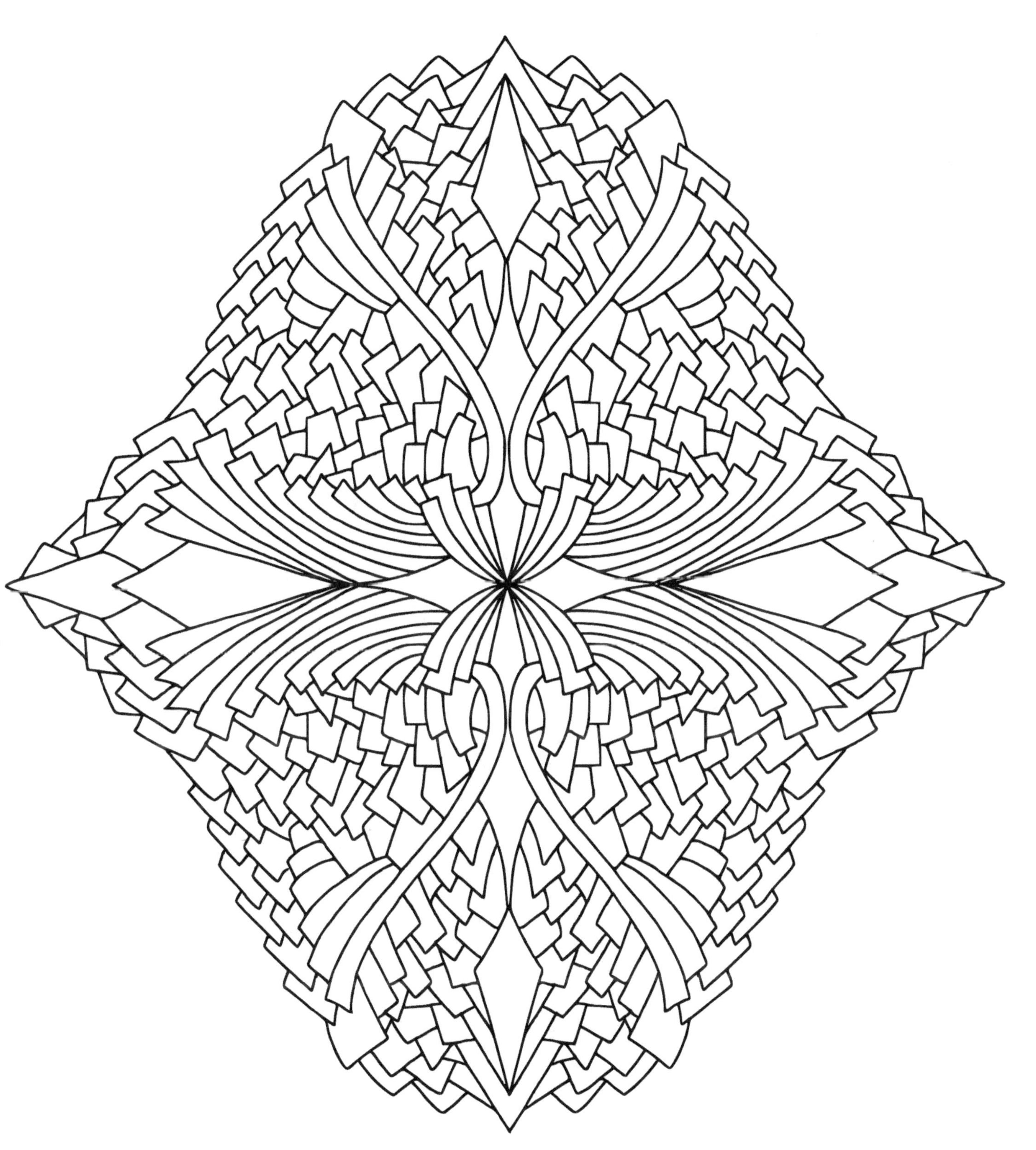

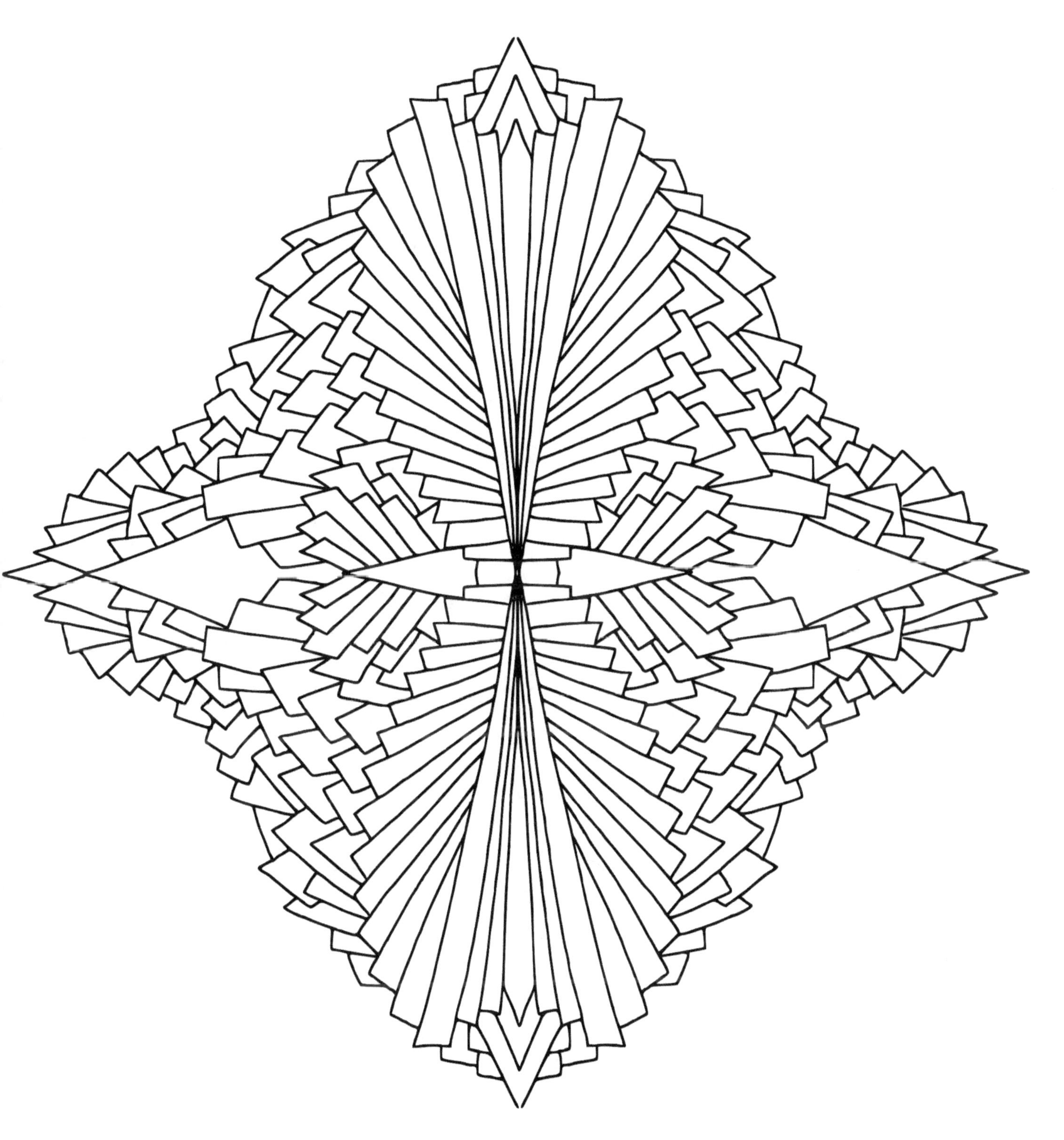

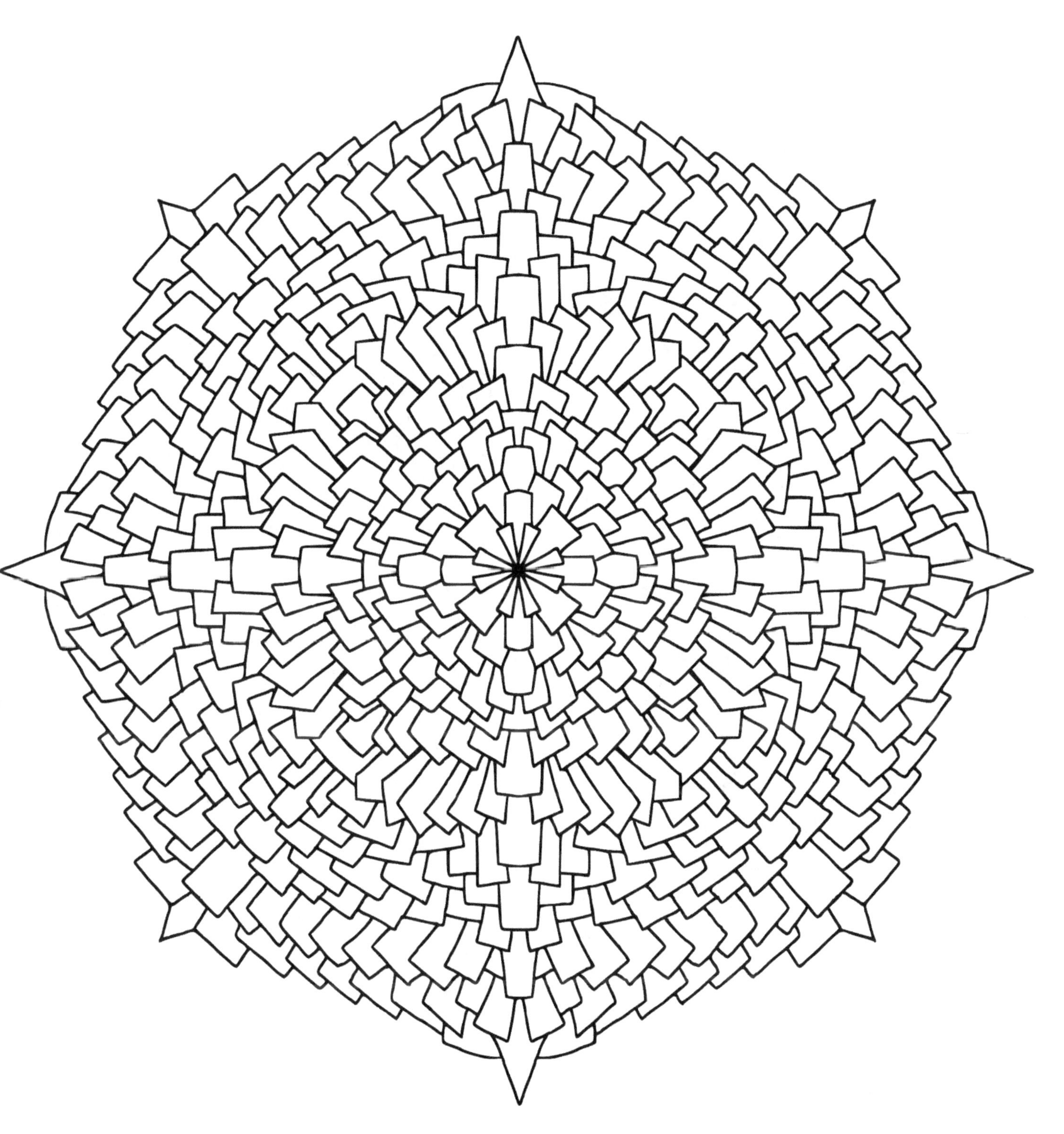

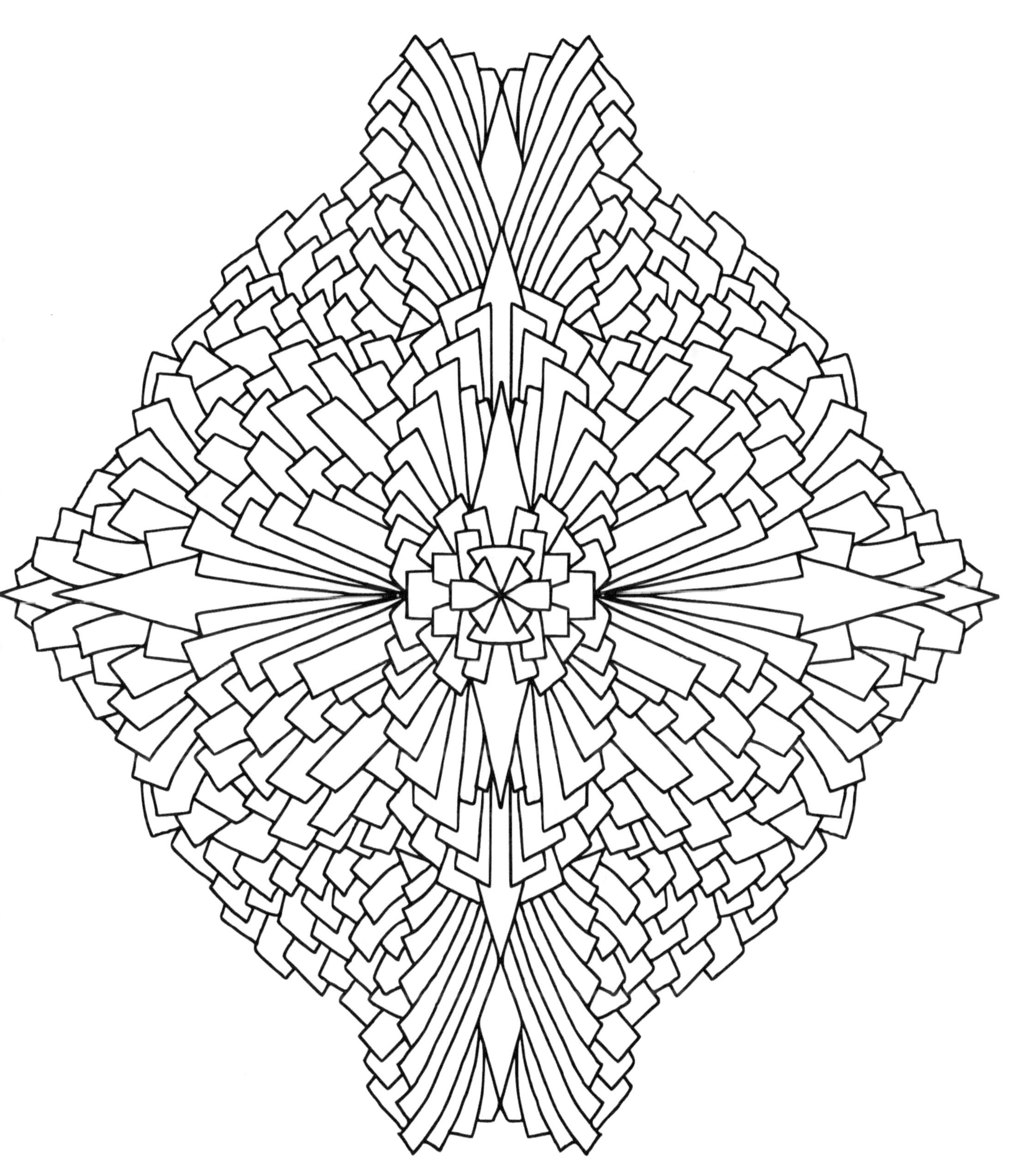

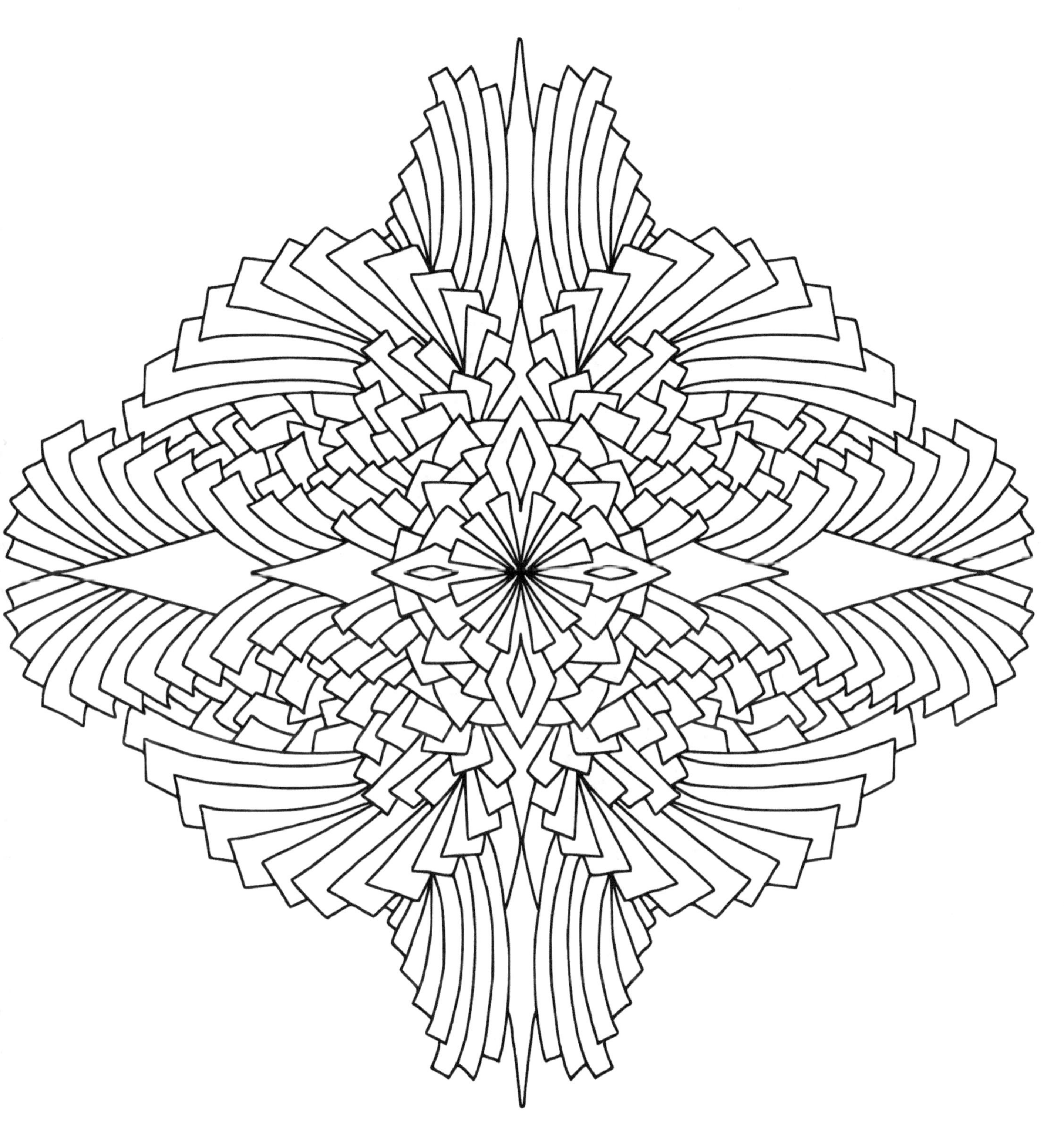

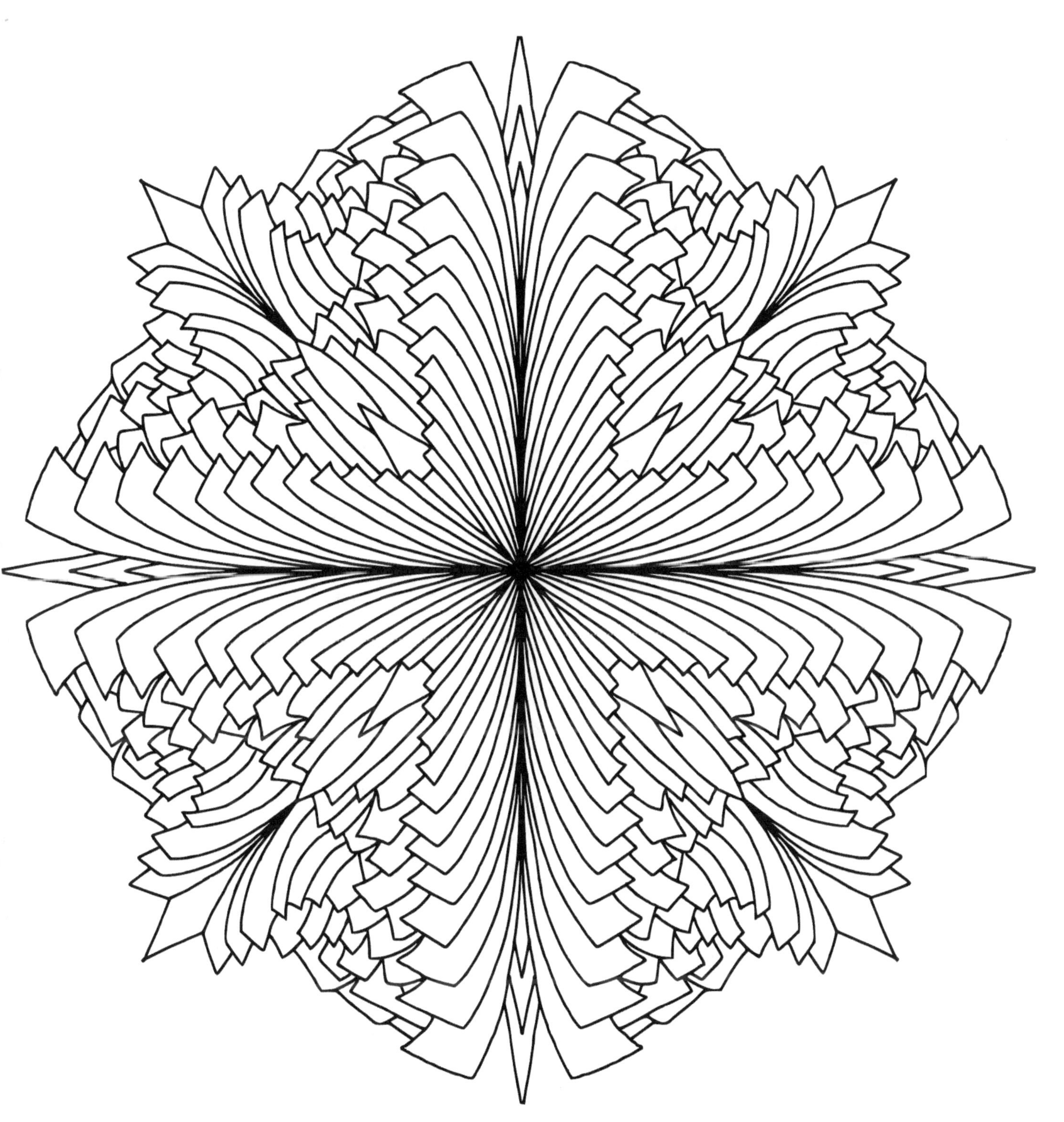

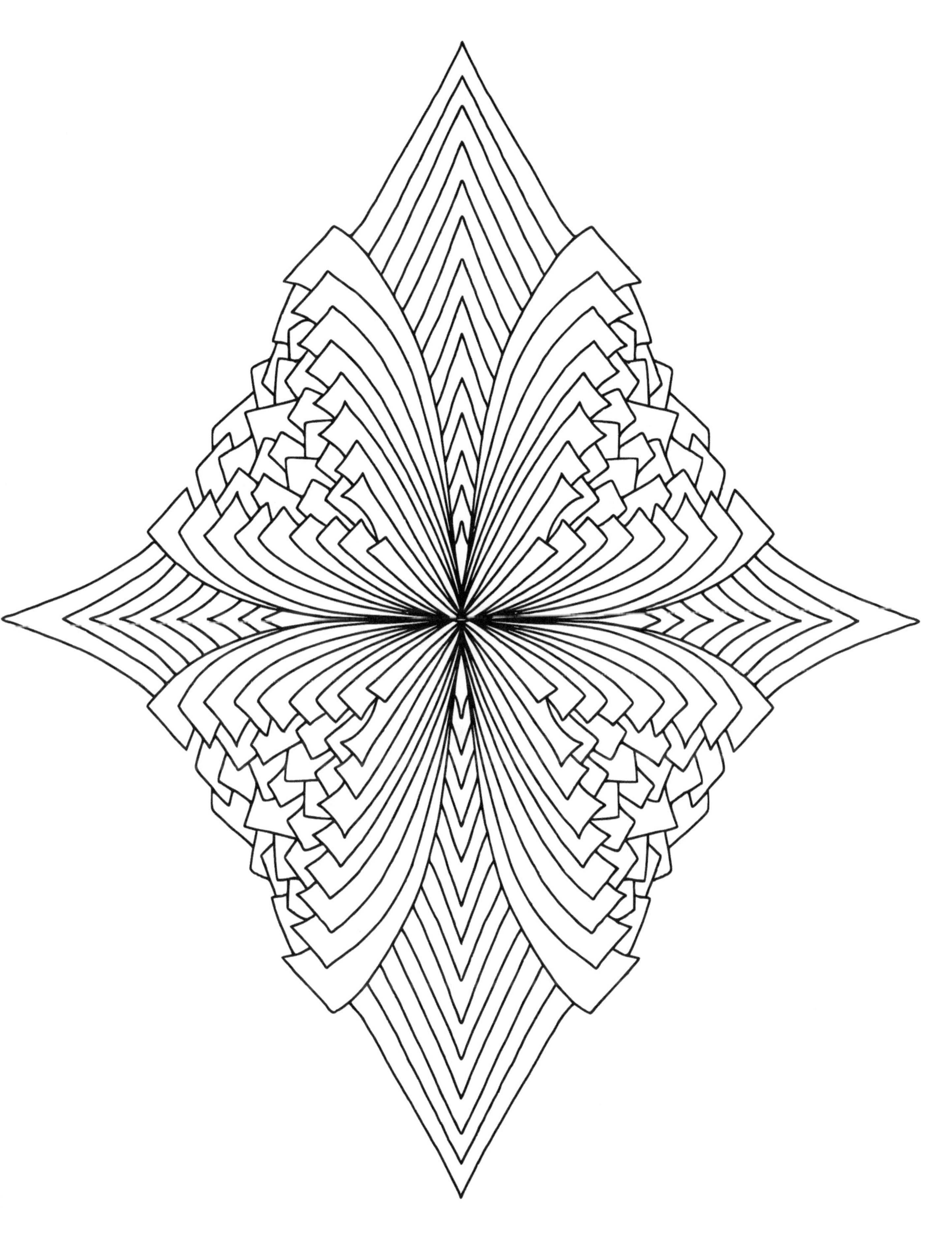

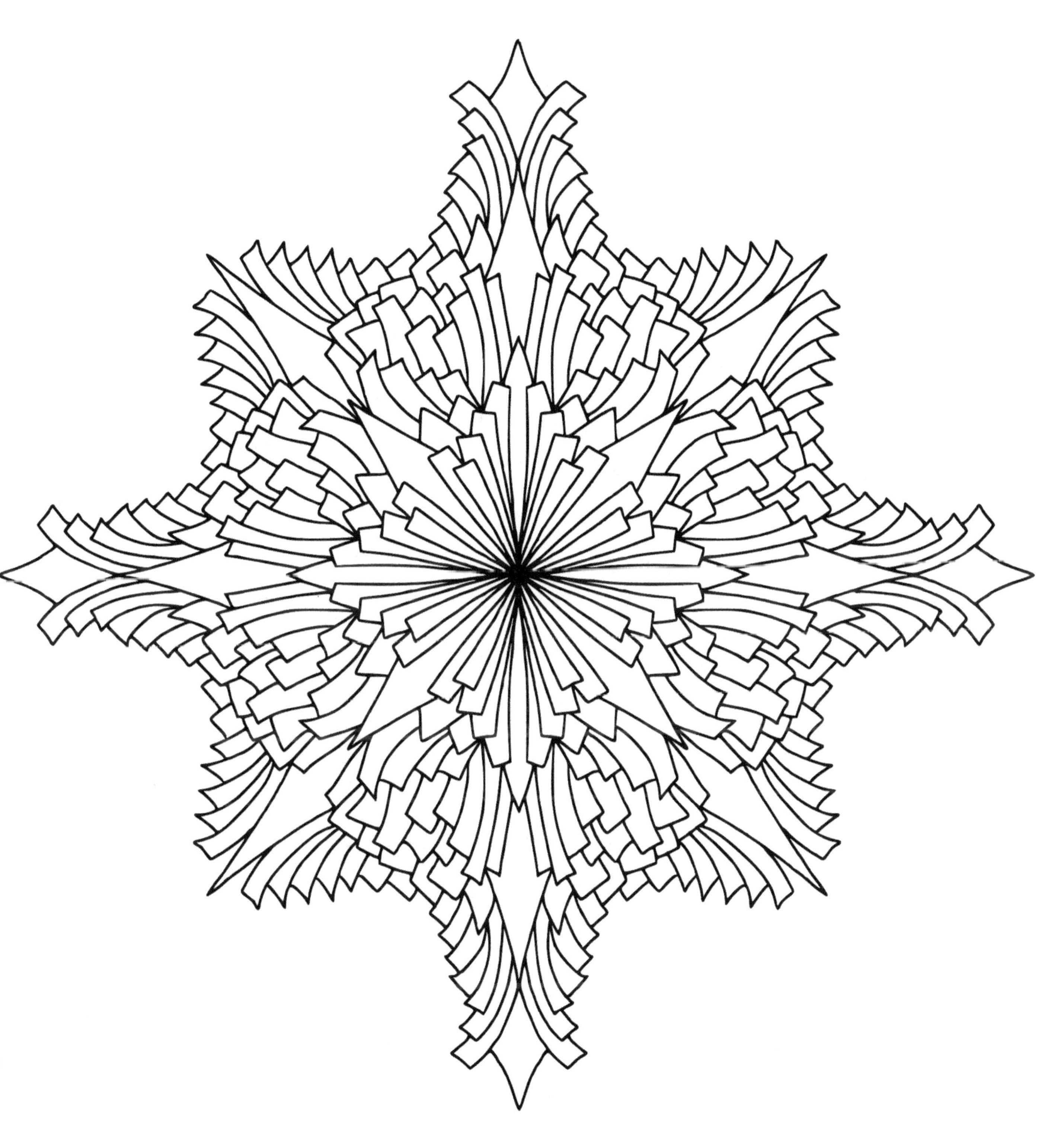

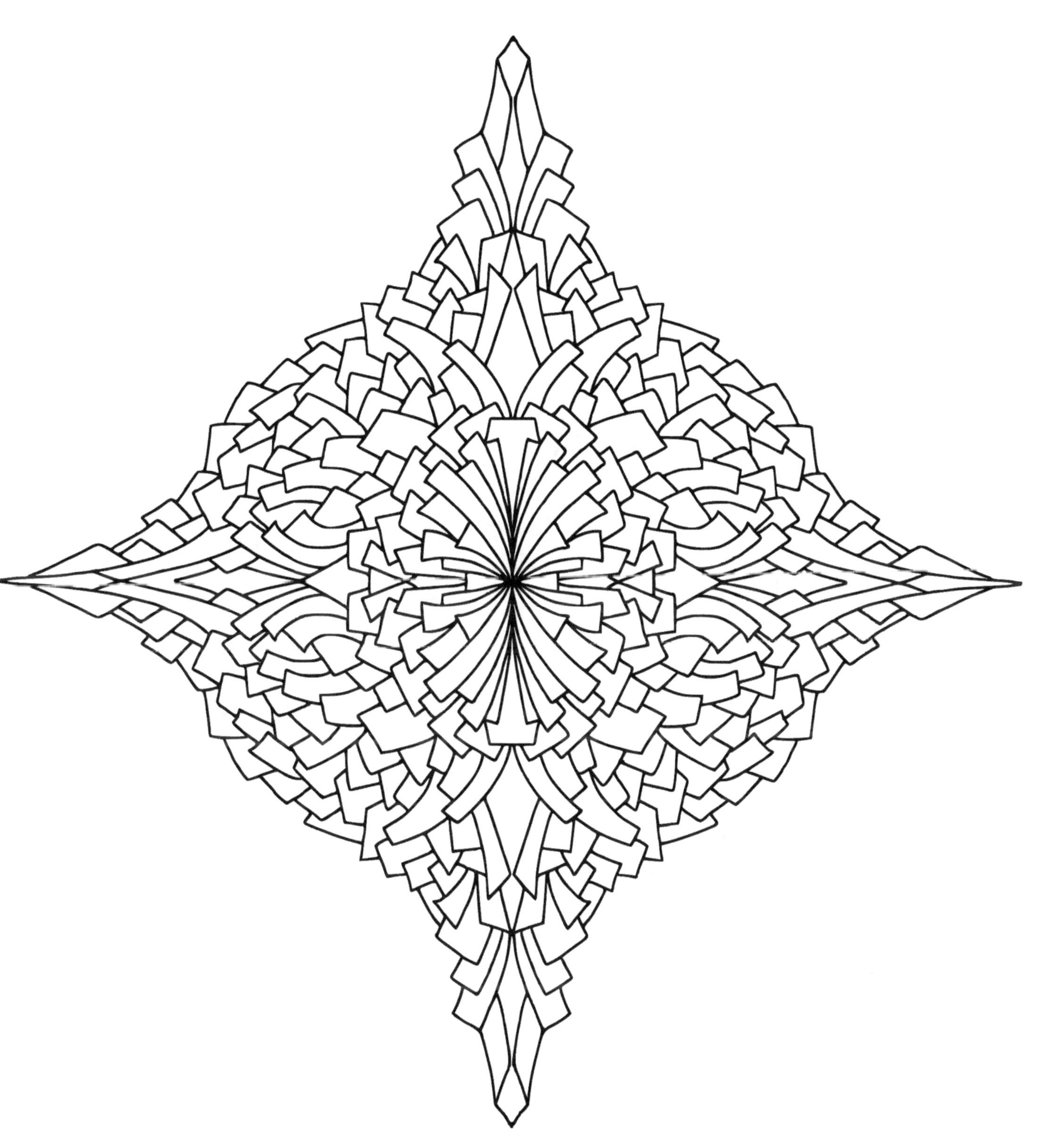

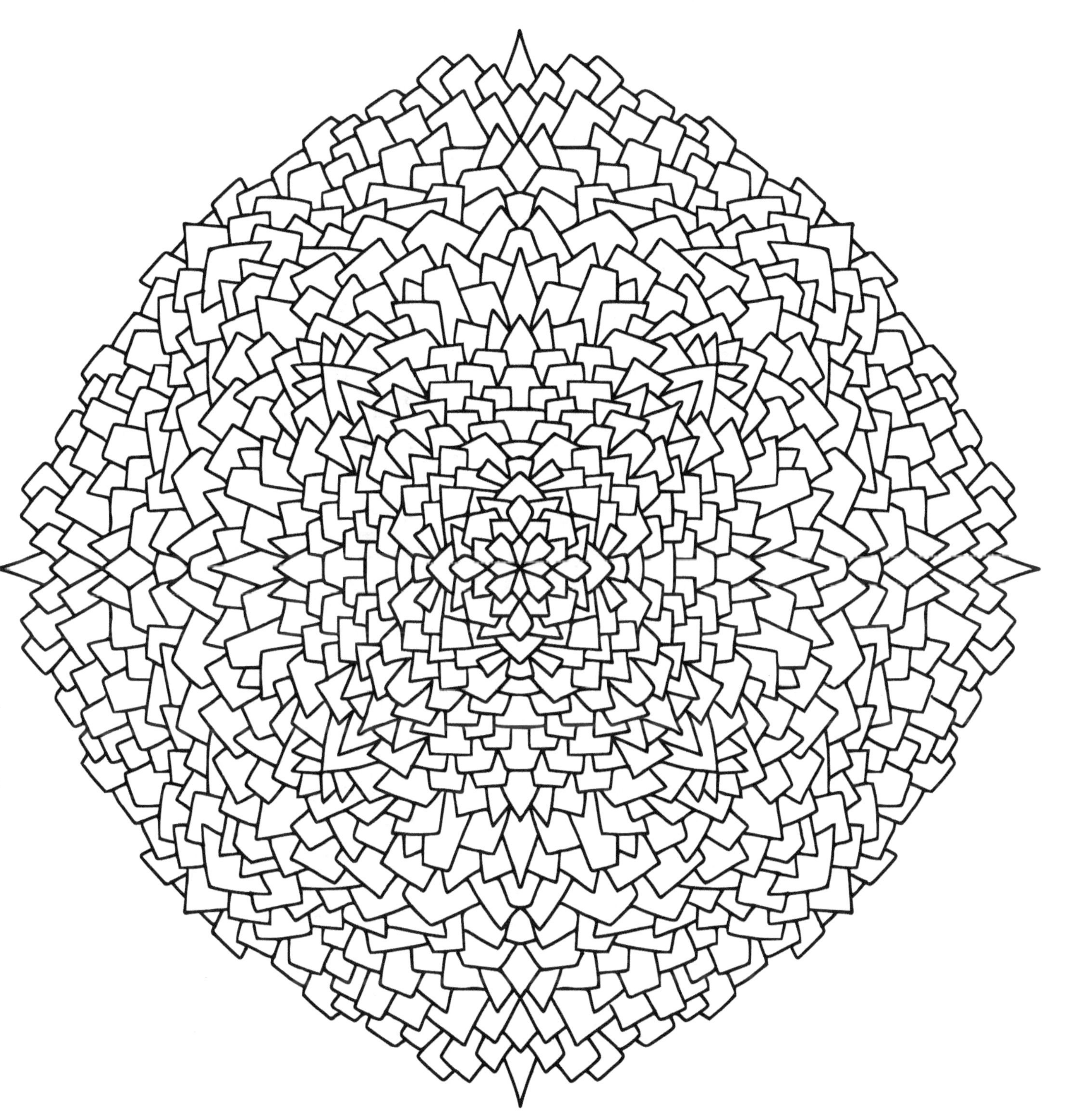

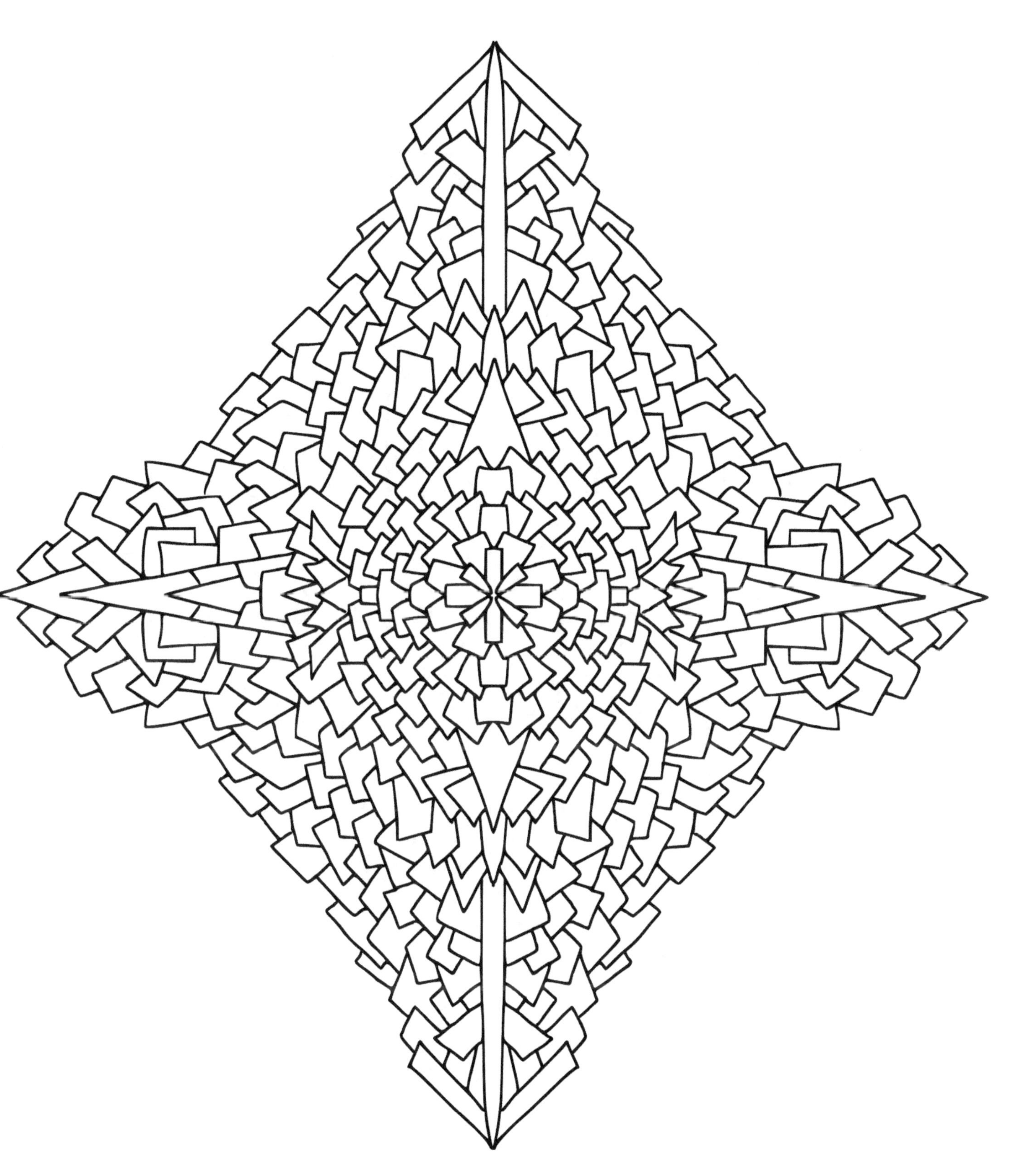

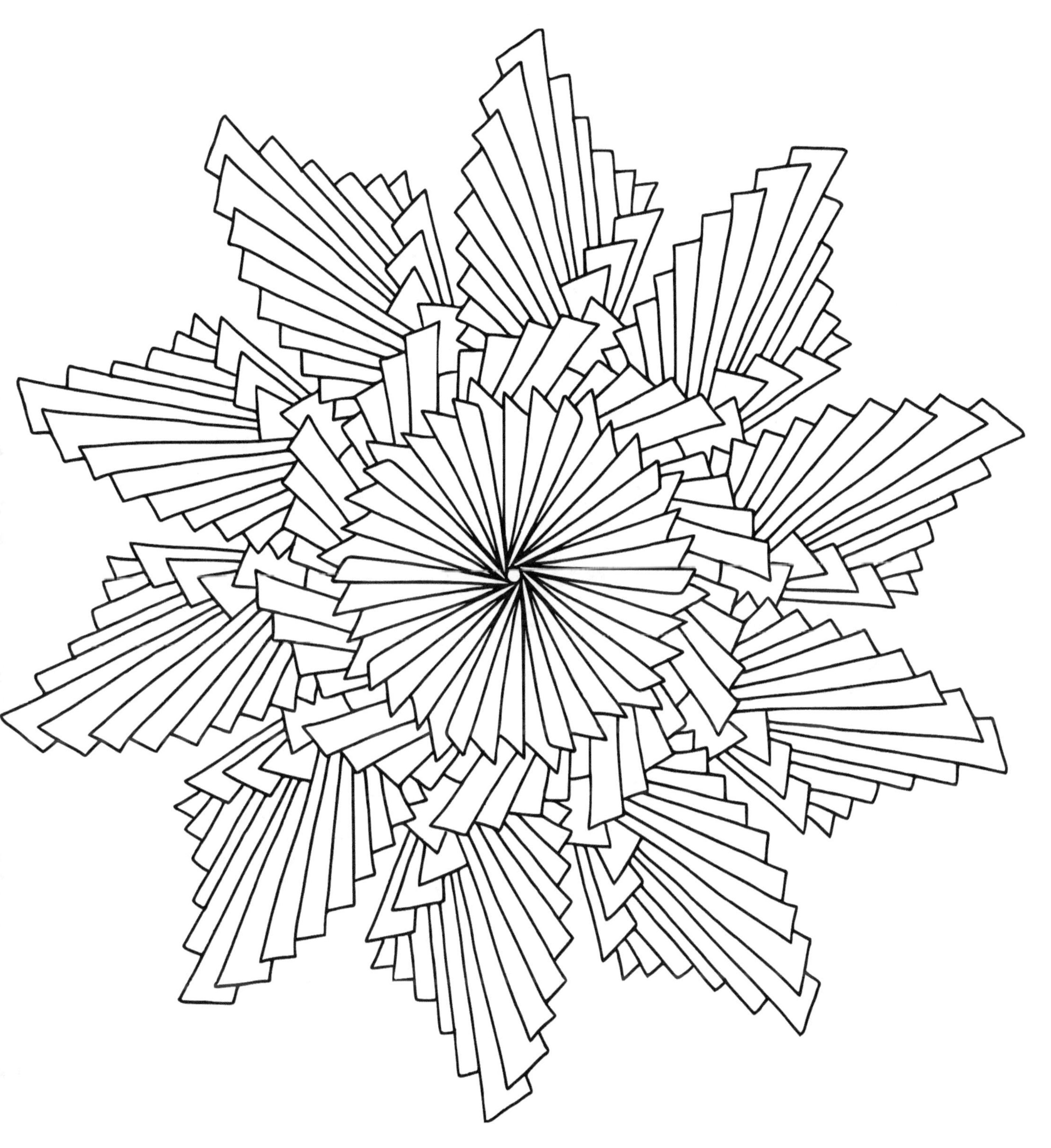

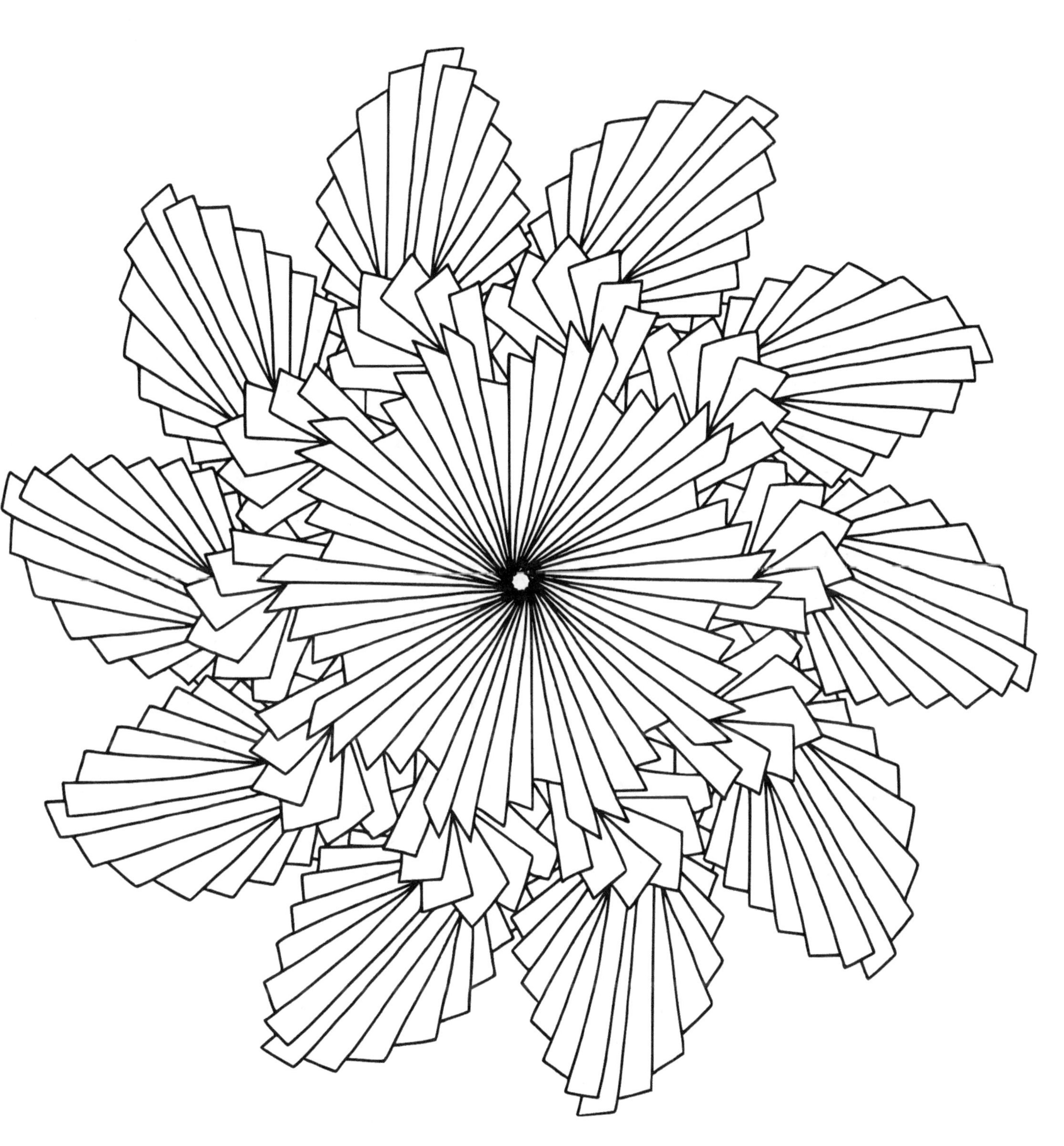

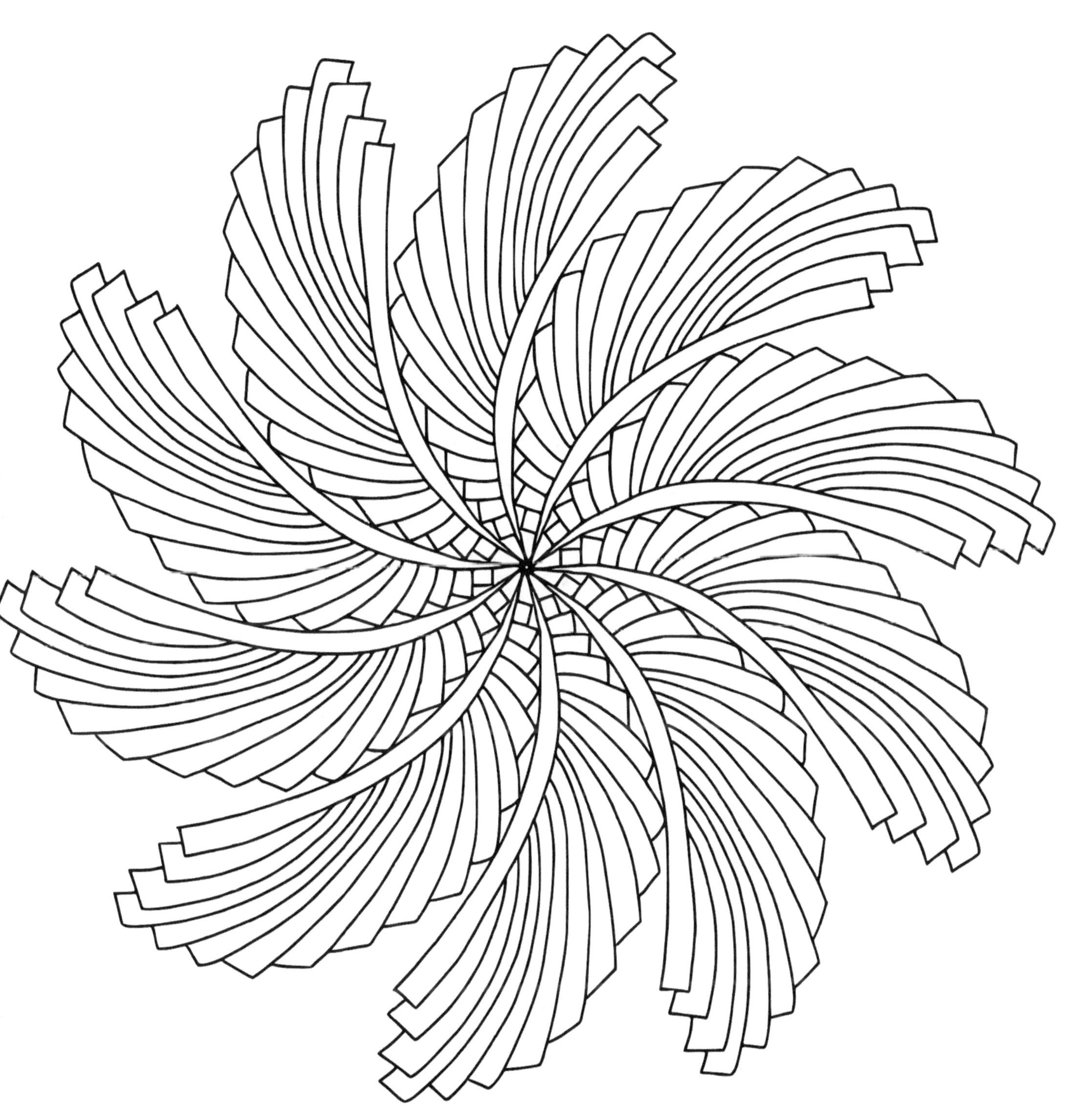

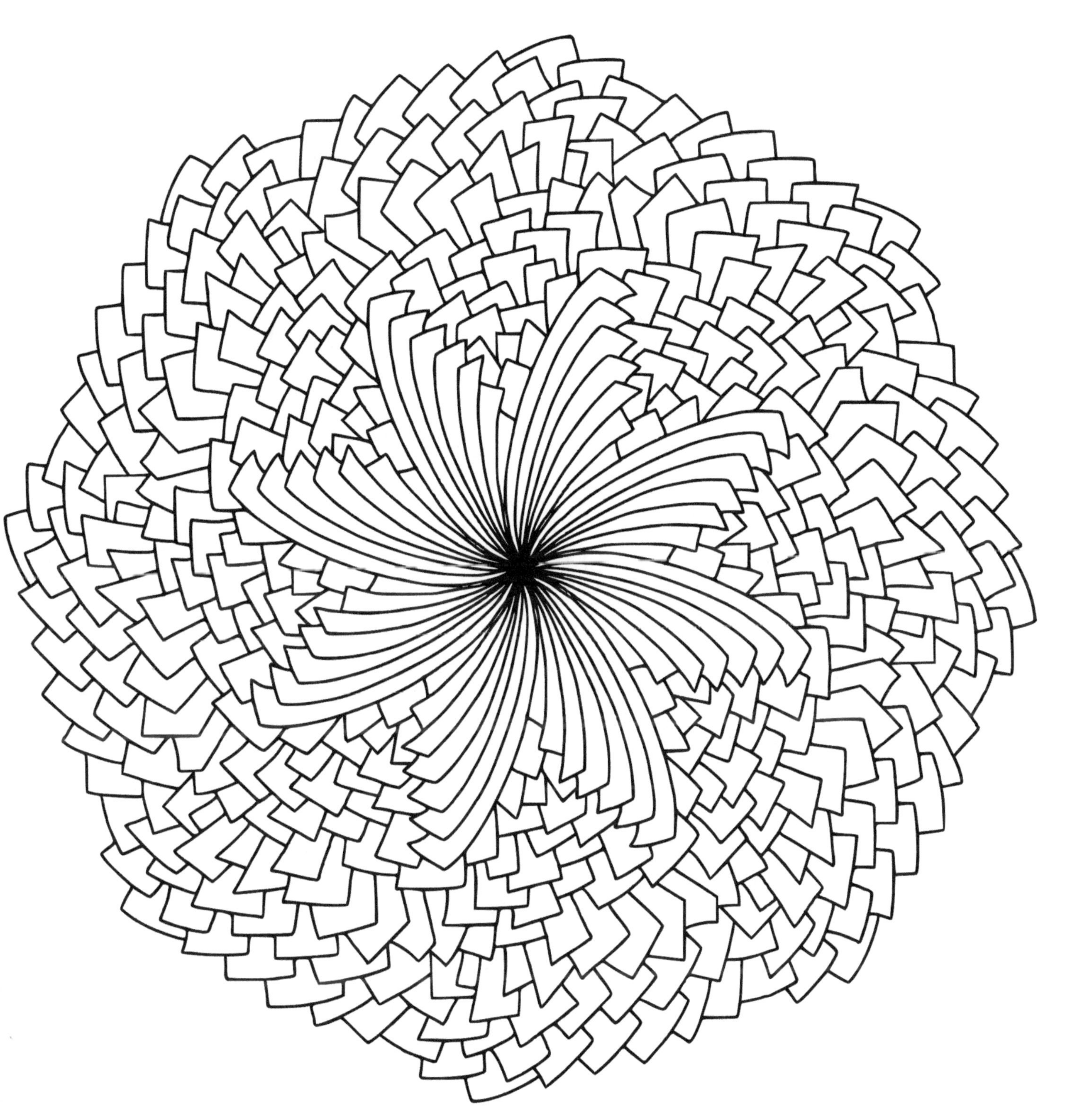

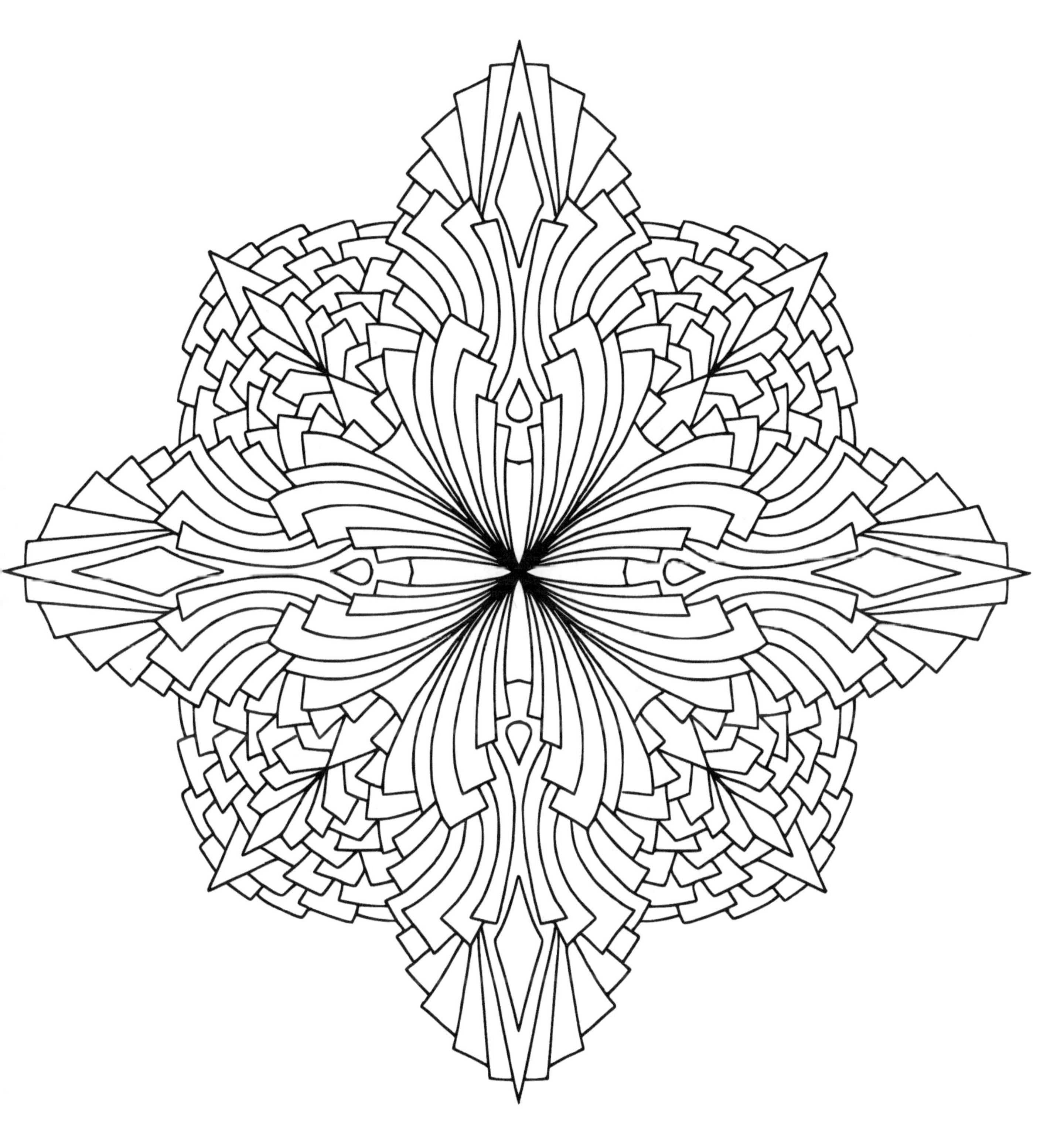

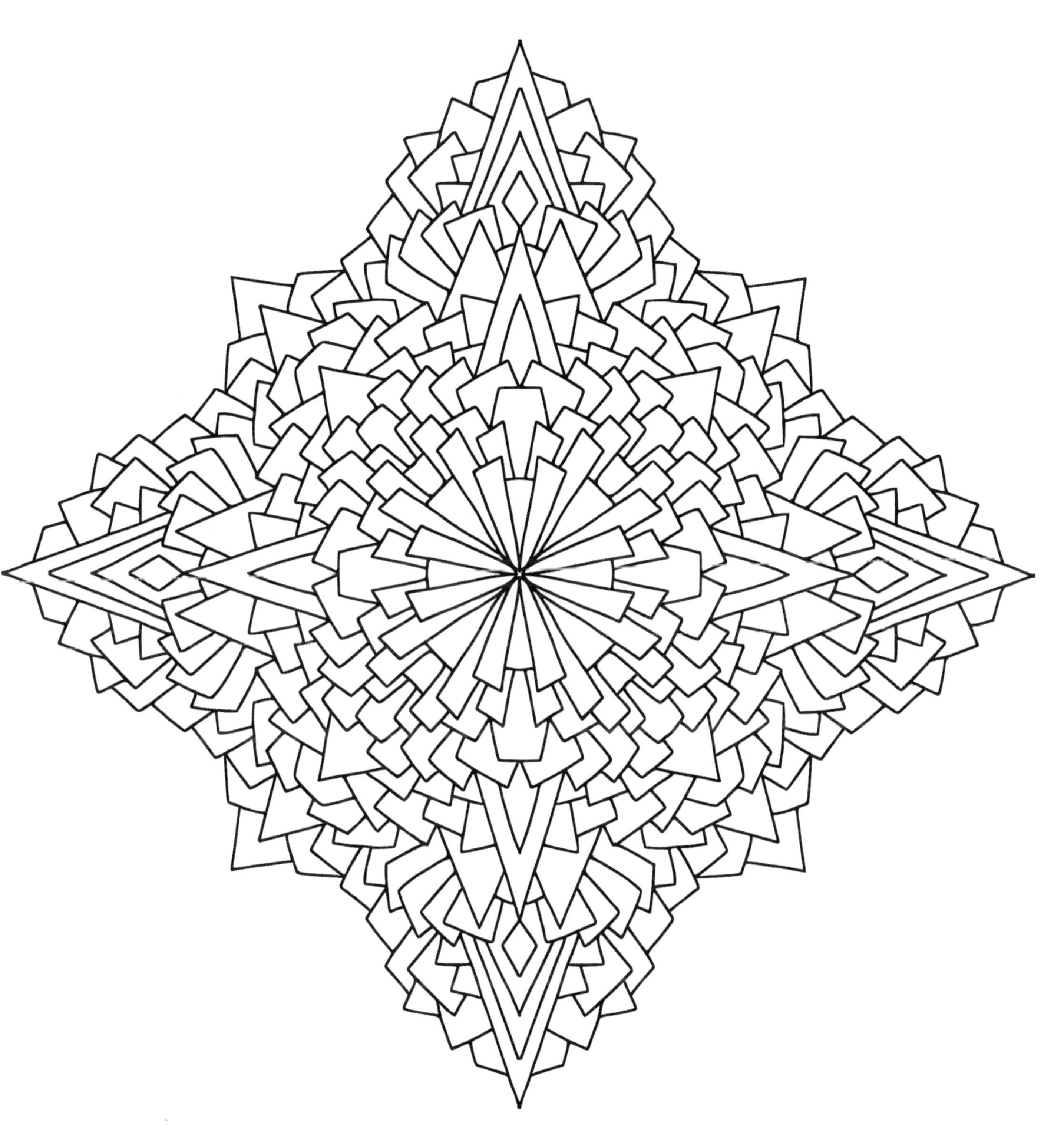

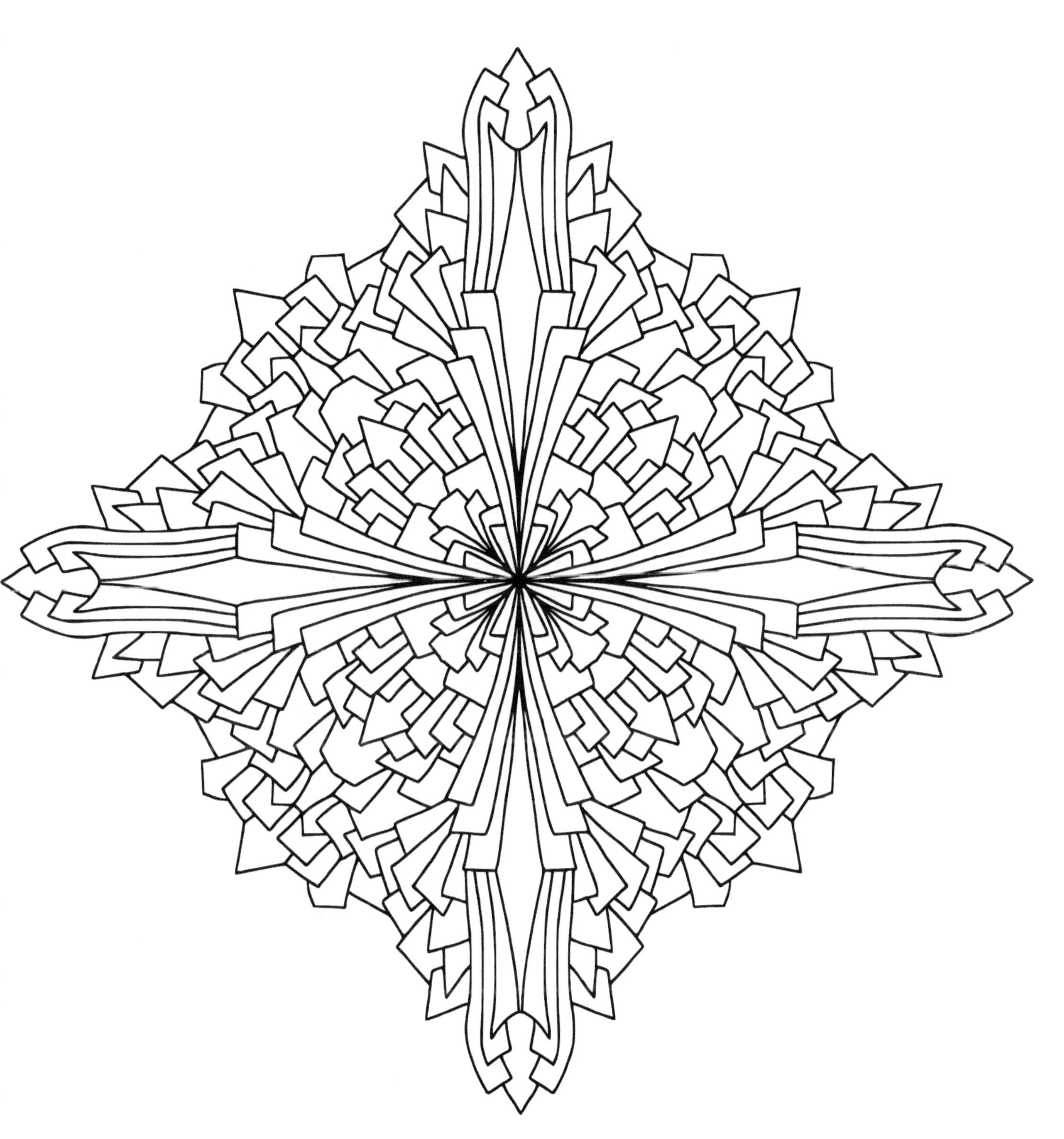

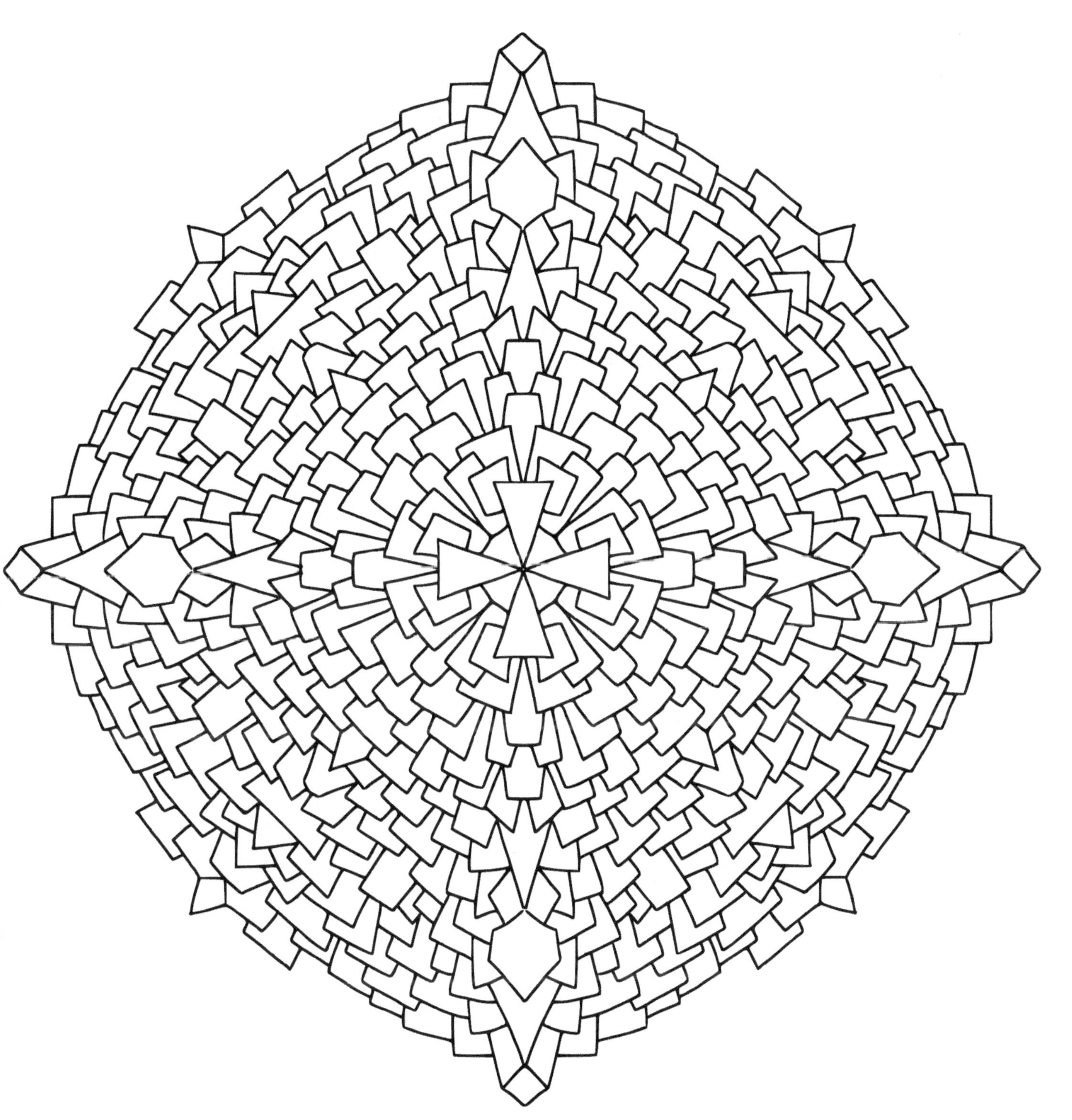

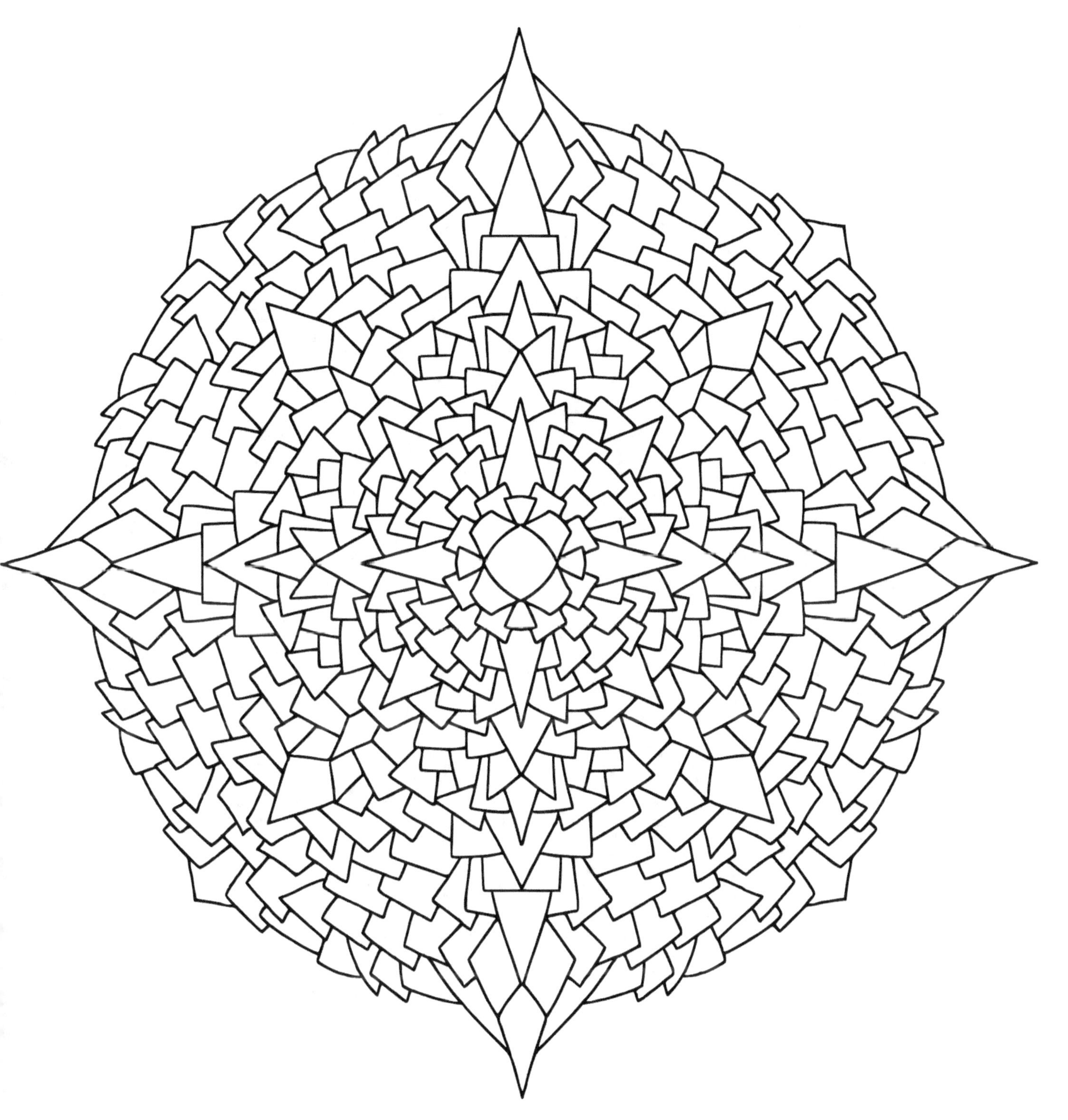

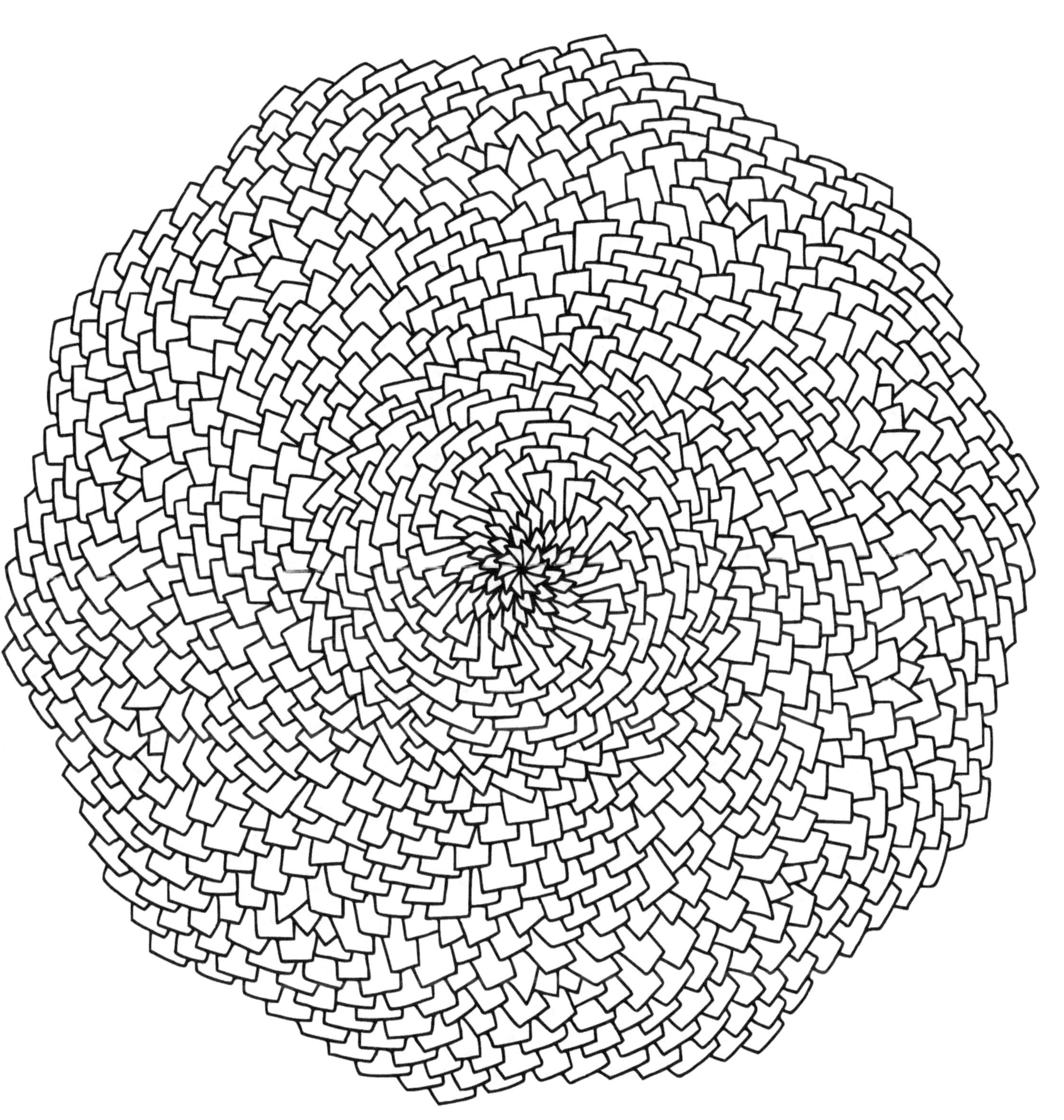

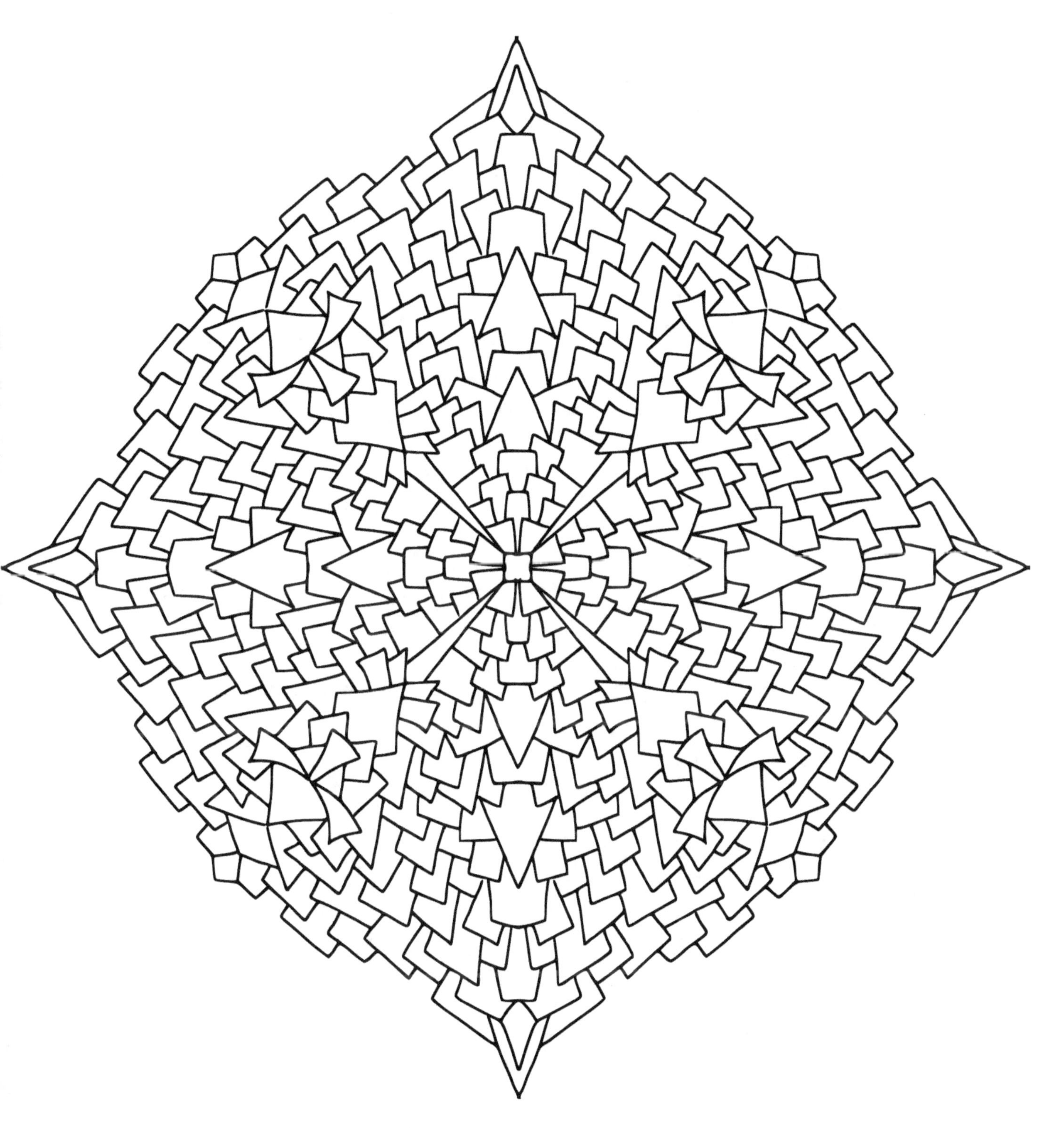

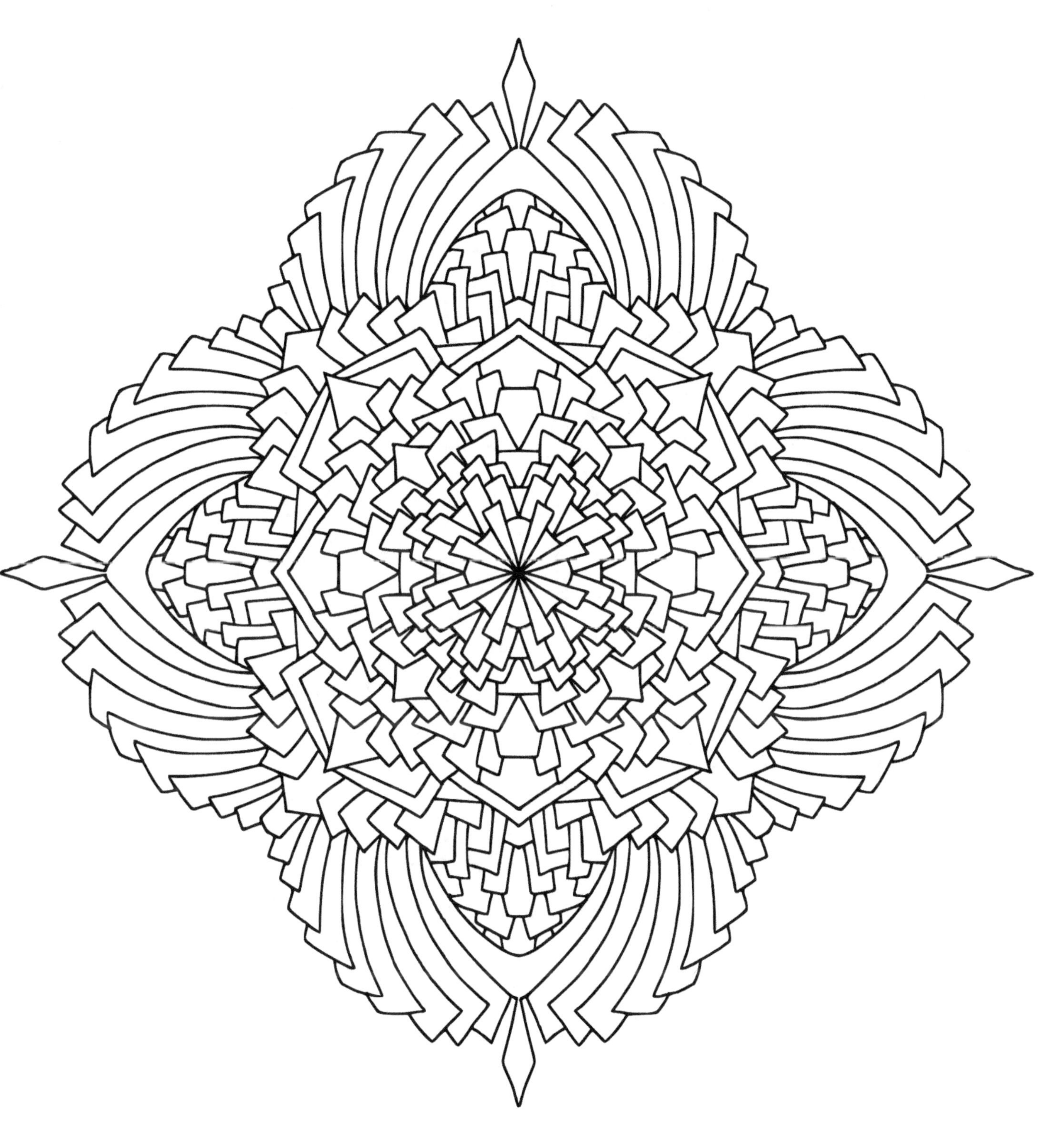

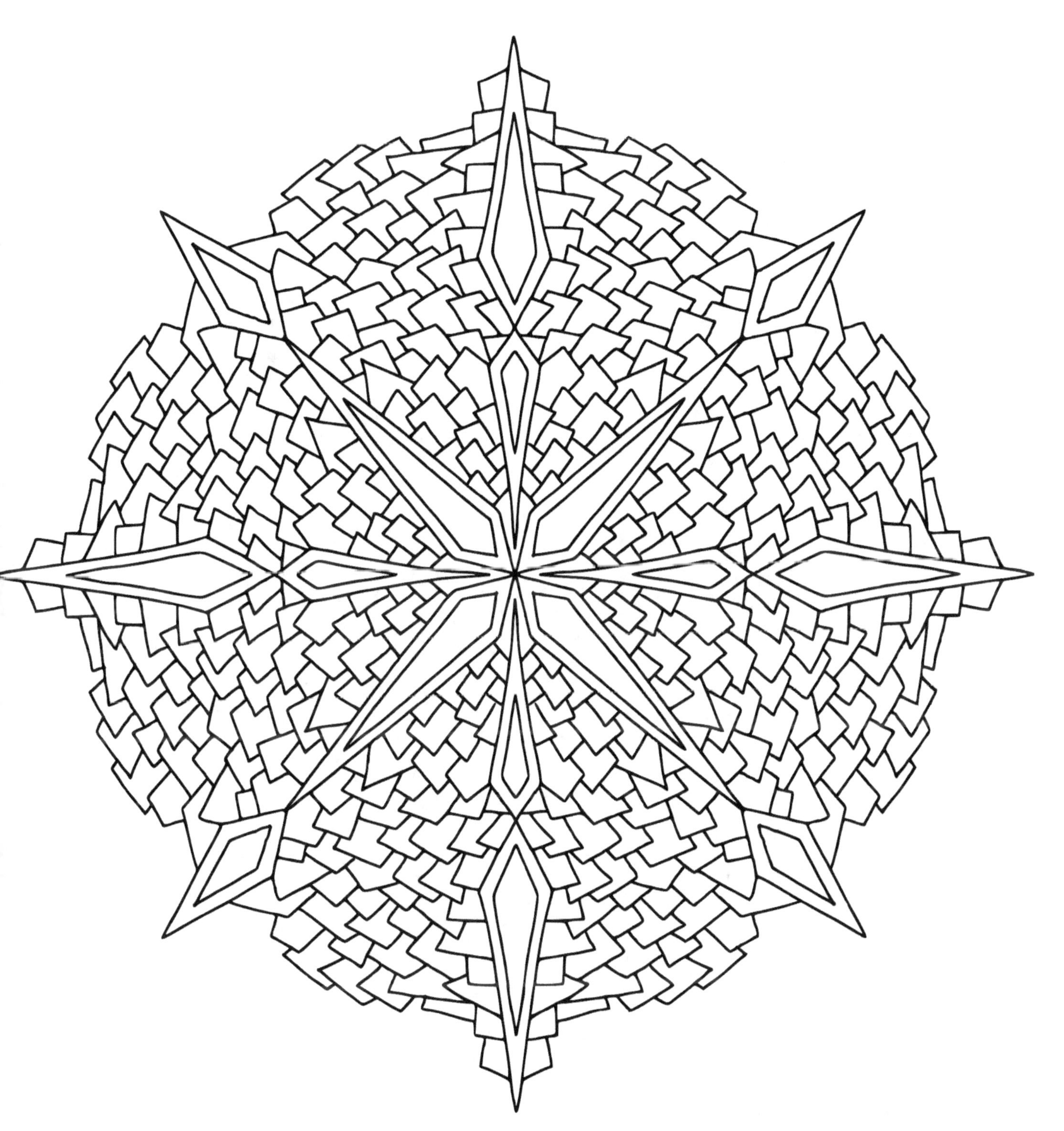

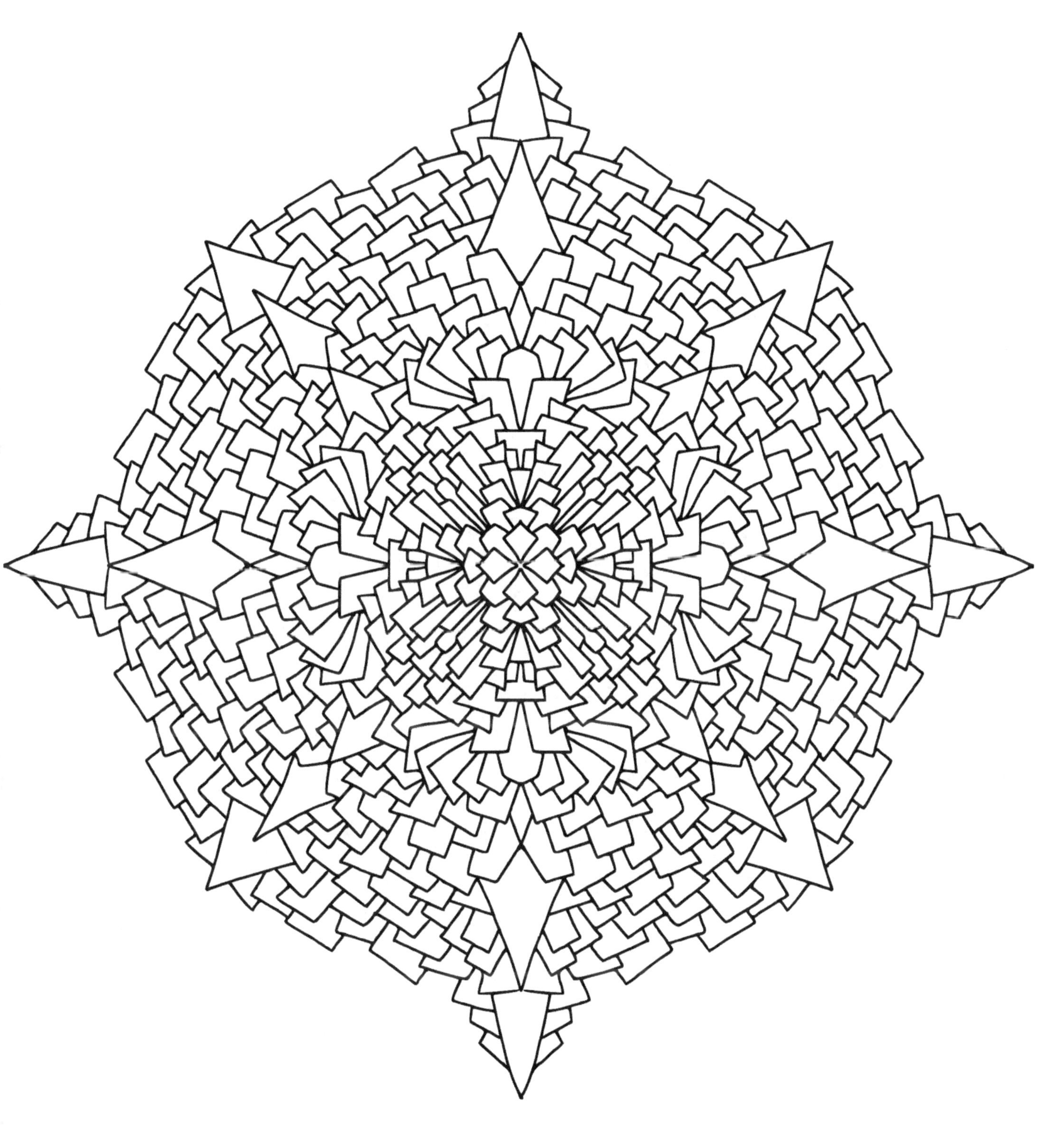

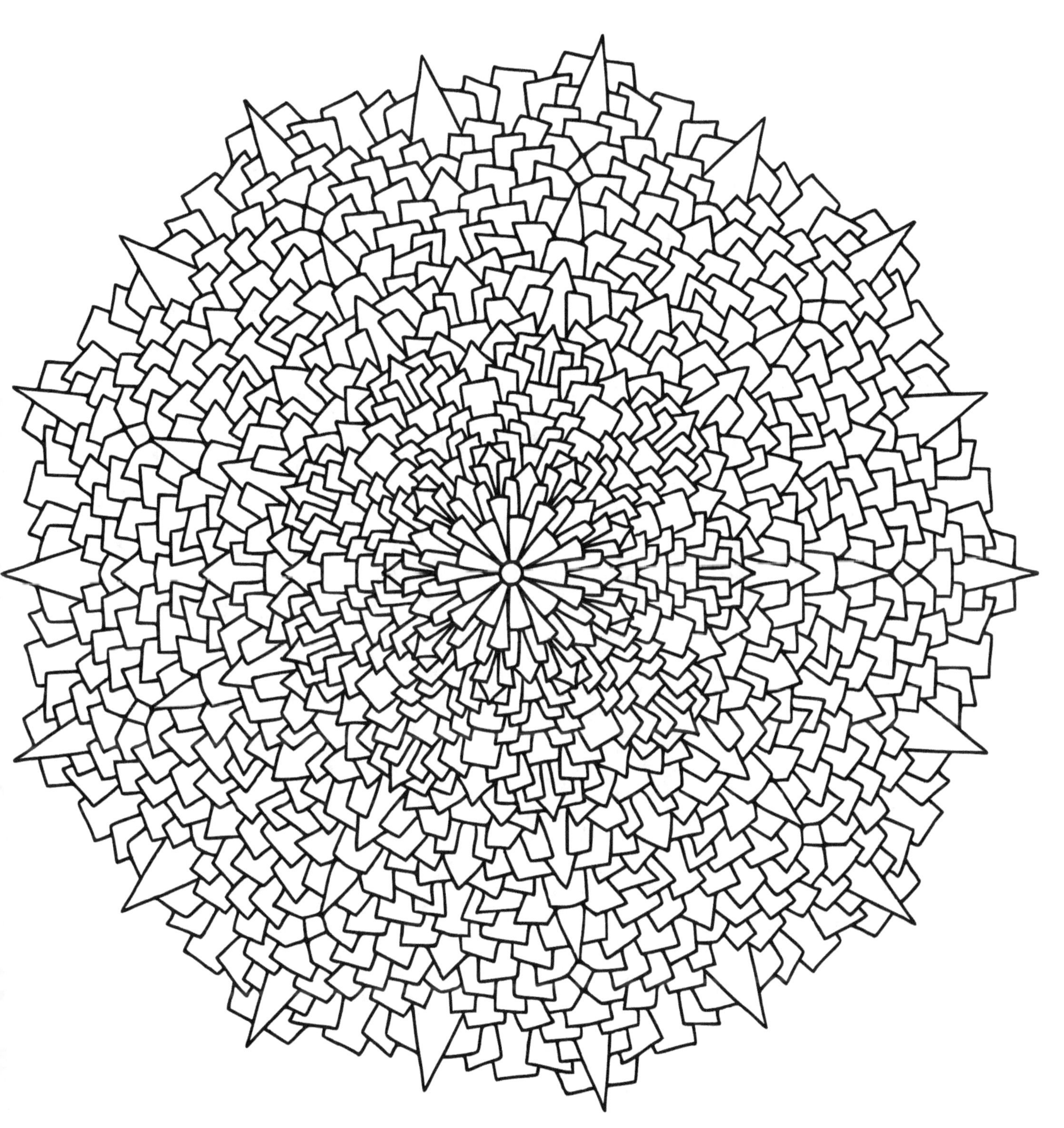

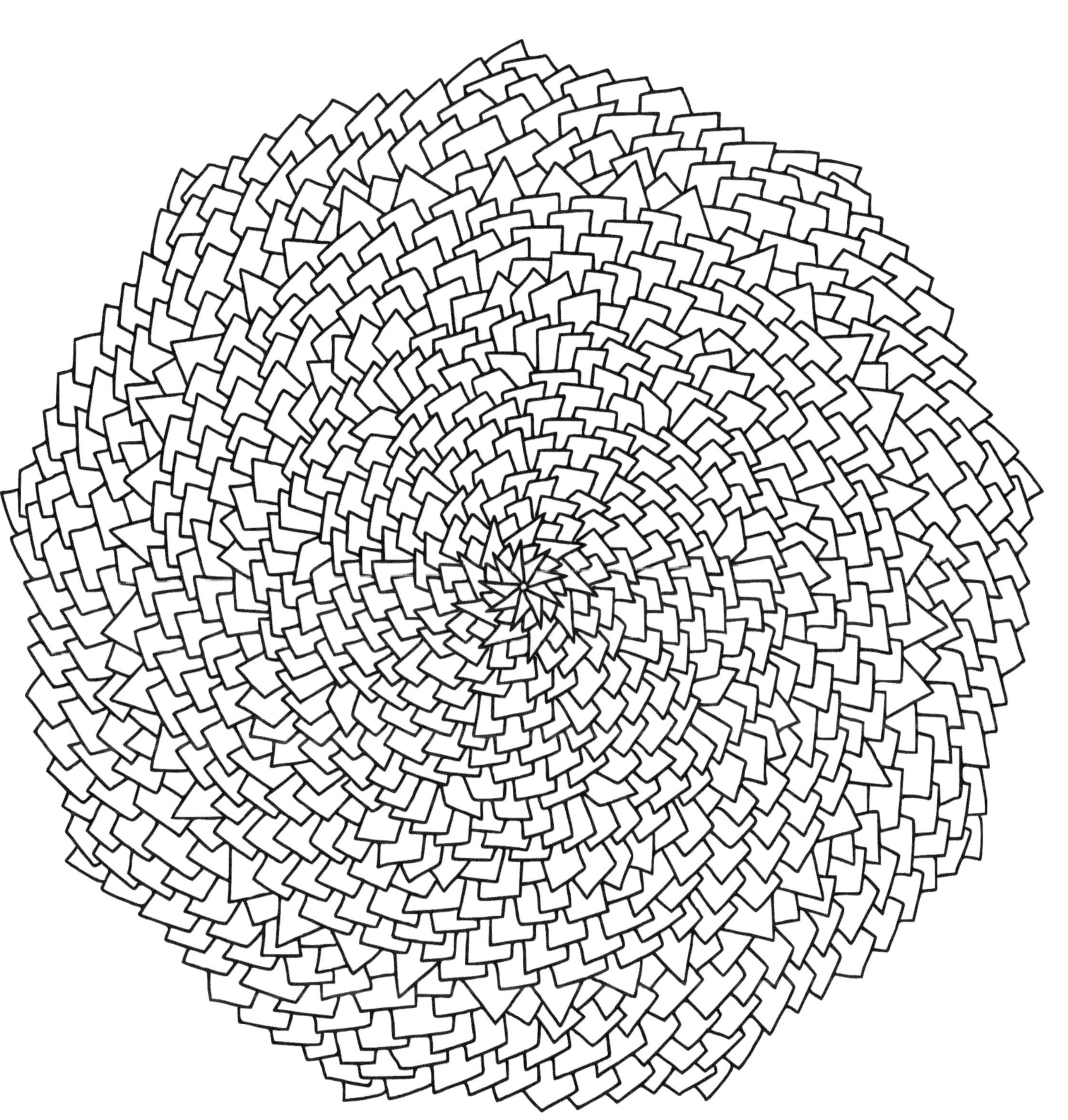

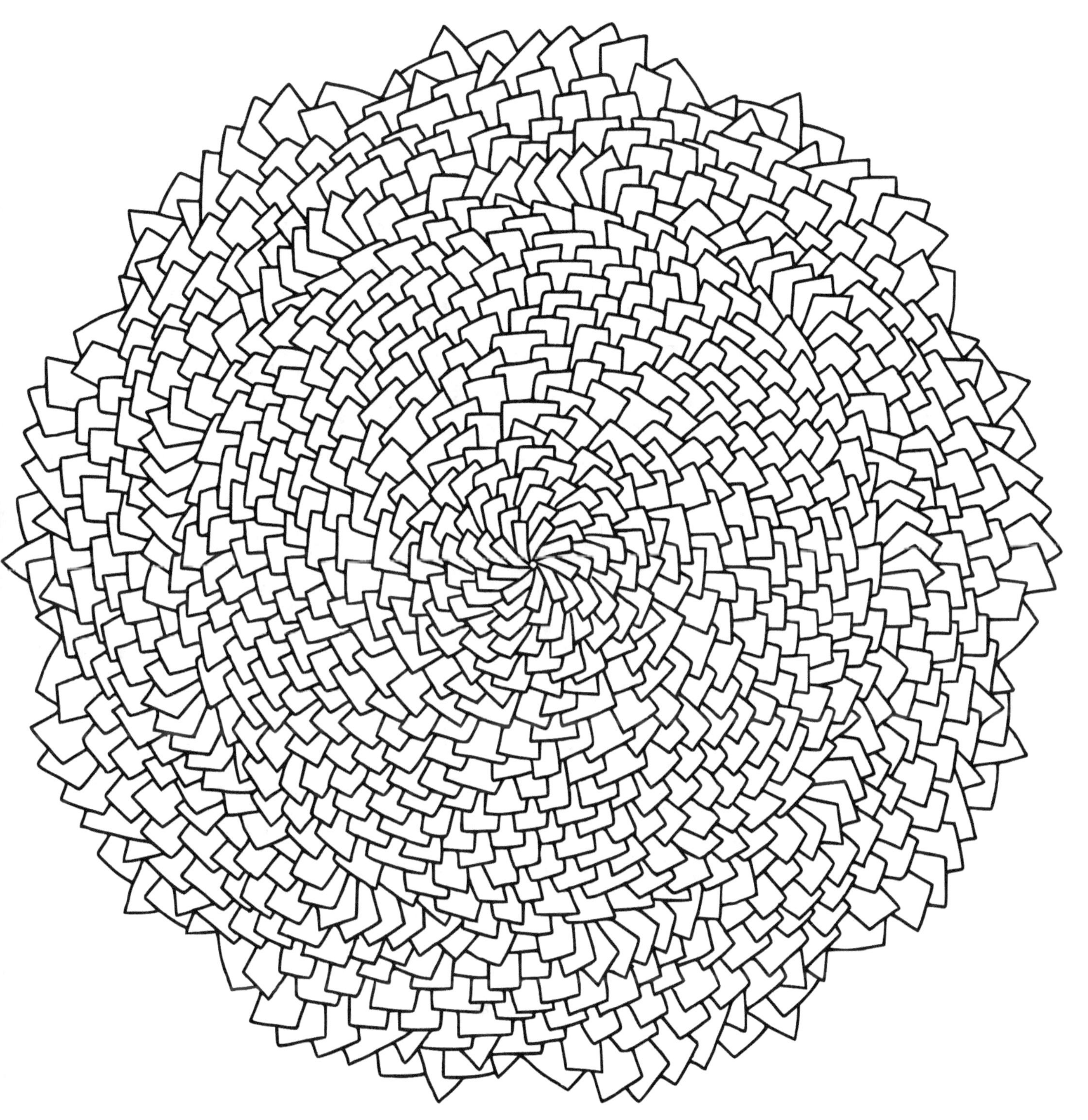

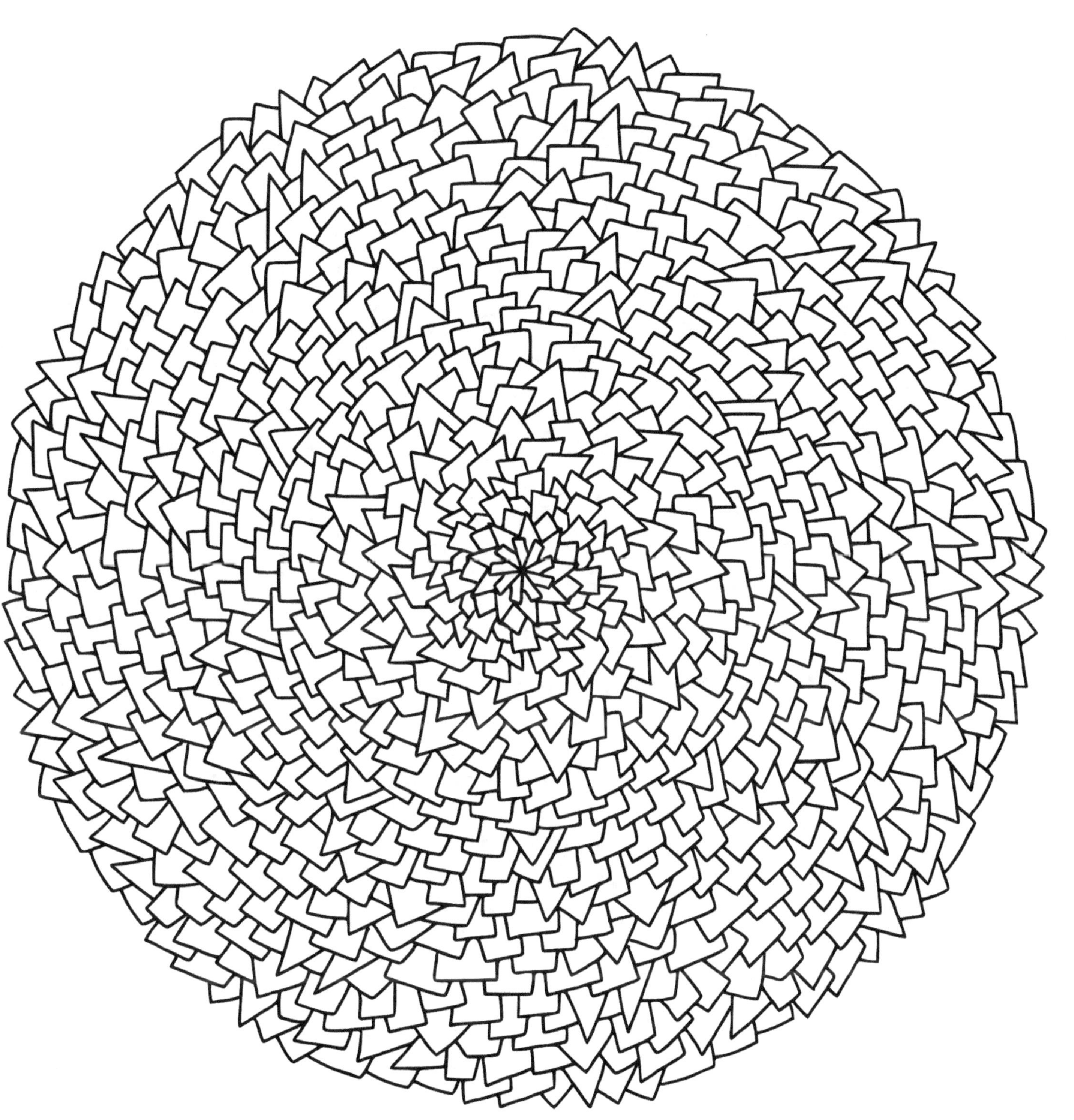

Test your colors here on the samples from
"My Pocket Coloring Companion"
&
"My Coloring Companion"

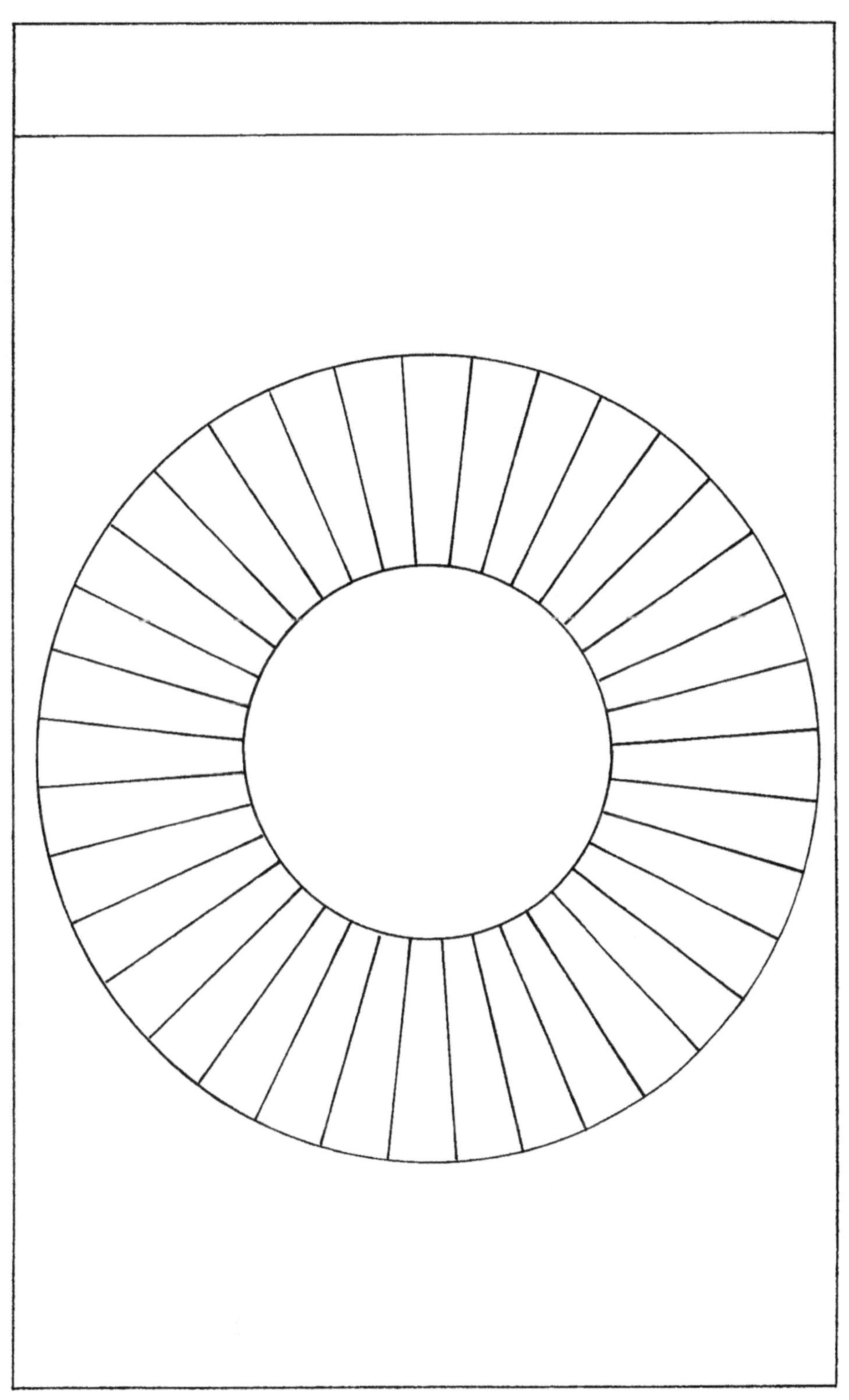

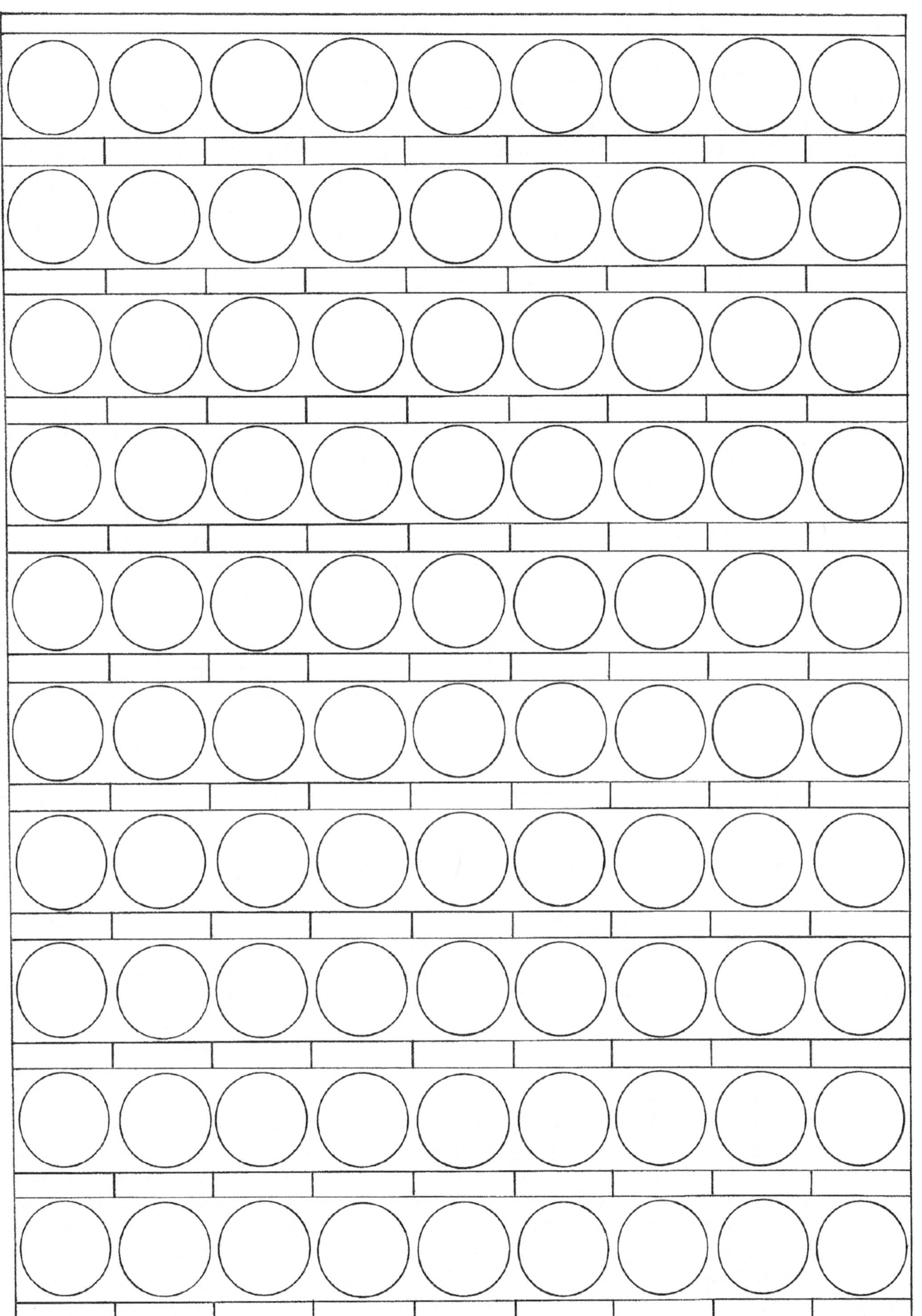